The Power of Habit Stacking

Change Management and Organizational Change

Corey Stephenson

In the ever-evolving landscape of business, organizations are constantly faced with the need to adapt and embrace change. Whether it's the introduction of new technologies, shifts in market dynamics, or internal restructuring, change management has become a crucial discipline for success. However, implementing change within an organization can be a complex and challenging process. That's where the concept of habit stacking comes into play – a powerful strategy that can catalyze change and drive organizational growth.

Change management, at its core, is about guiding individuals, teams, and entire organizations through the process of transition. It entails understanding the current state, envisioning the desired future state, and strategically bridging the gap between them. While change can be disruptive and met with resistance, it also presents opportunities for innovation, improvement, and competitive advantage.

Enter habit stacking, a concept rooted in the understanding that lasting change is often best achieved by leveraging existing habits and routines. Habit stacking involves building upon existing behaviors to create new, desired habits. It recognizes that humans are creatures of habit, and by consciously linking new actions to established ones, the likelihood of successful adoption and integration increases significantly.

In the context of organizations, habit stacking can be a transformative tool for change management. It acknowledges that change is not a one-time event but rather an ongoing process. By identifying and capitalizing on existing routines and habits within the organizational culture, leaders can introduce and embed new behaviors, processes, and mindsets more effectively.

Consider the example of implementing a new project management software within a company. The change may be met with skepticism and resistance from employees accustomed to traditional methods. However, by employing habit stacking, the organization can tap into existing habits, such as daily team meetings, and integrate the new software seamlessly. By linking the use of the software to the habitual meetings, employees can gradually adapt to the change and see the value it brings to their existing routines.

Furthermore, habit stacking not only facilitates change but also promotes sustainability. When new behaviors become ingrained as habits, they are more likely to endure beyond the initial implementation phase. This creates a culture of continuous improvement and adaptability, where change becomes an inherent part of the organization's DNA.

However, effective habit stacking requires thoughtful planning, clear communication, and leadership commitment. It involves identifying the critical behaviors that need to change, understanding the existing habits and routines, and strategically integrating new behaviors into the organizational fabric.

In the following pages, we will delve deeper into the principles and strategies of change management and habit stacking. We will explore real-life case studies of organizations that have successfully utilized habit stacking to drive meaningful change. Additionally, we will provide practical tools and frameworks to help leaders navigate the complexities of change management and harness the power of habit stacking within their organizations.

Change is inevitable in the dynamic world of business. By embracing change management and harnessing the power of habit stacking, organizations can not only survive but also thrive in an ever-changing landscape. The journey towards organizational transformation begins here.

Contact Me

I'd love to hear more about your experiences and success.

EMAIL ME:

coreystephenson@coreystephenson.com

FIND ME:

https://www.facebook.com/corey.murteza

JOIN US:

https://www.facebook.com/groups/EntrepreneurHer

One of my fundamental beliefs is that we all need support and community in this crazy journey we call entrepreneurship.

LET'S TALK:

If you are interested in setting up a one-on-one call with me, please go to www.coreystephenson.com. I can't wait to meet you!

MORE TITLES FROM COREY STEPHENSON...
The Power of Habit Stacking

https://books2read.com/u/4jNkP5

Achieving personal growth and making positive changes in our lives can be challenging. We often find ourselves overwhelmed by a multitude of goals and aspirations, unsure of where to start or how to sustain our efforts. This is where habit stacking comes in—a powerful technique that can revolutionize the way we approach behavior change and enable us to create lasting habits that propel us towards success.

Habit Stacking for Kids: Instilling Lifelong Habits Effectively

https://books2read.com/u/3GpB6P

Habits play a significant role in shaping our lives, and this holds true for children as well. From the moment they wake up to the time they go to bed, children engage in a multitude of habits that influence their behavior, learning, and overall well-being. We will explore the power of habits in shaping a child's life and how they contribute to long-term success.

TABLE OF CONTENTS

CHAPTER 1

The Importance of Change Management in Organizations

Change is a constant in today's dynamic business environment. Organizations face numerous internal and external factors that necessitate change, such as technological advancements, market shifts, competitive pressures, and evolving customer expectations. However, managing change effectively is a complex endeavor that requires a structured approach. This chapter explores the importance of change management in organizations and highlights why it is crucial for long-term success.

Understanding Change Management

Change management is the discipline and process of guiding individuals, teams, and entire organizations through a planned transition from the current state to a desired future state. It involves identifying the need for change, creating a vision, developing strategies, and implementing interventions to support individuals and teams in adapting to the change. Change management encompasses both the human and organizational aspects of transformation, ensuring that employees are engaged, equipped, and empowered throughout the process.

The Impact of Change Management

Minimizing Resistance: Change often disrupts established routines, creates uncertainty, and can lead to resistance from employees. Effective change management helps mitigate resistance by providing a structured approach that includes clear communication, involvement, and support. By involving employees in the change process and addressing their concerns, organizations can minimize resistance and increase the likelihood of successful implementation.

Maximizing Adoption: Change initiatives can only be successful if they are adopted and integrated into the fabric of the organization. Change management strategies provide a framework for fostering adoption by engaging employees and providing them with the necessary resources and training to embrace the change. When employees understand the benefits and have the tools to navigate the transition, they are more likely to adopt new behaviors, processes, and technologies.

Enhancing Employee Engagement: Change can create anxiety and uncertainty among employees, impacting morale and productivity. Change management focuses on creating a supportive and inclusive environment where employees feel valued, involved, and motivated. By involving employees in decision-making, providing training and development opportunities, and recognizing their contributions, organizations can enhance employee engagement and maintain productivity during times of change.

Aligning Organizational Objectives: Change management ensures that organizational change initiatives are aligned with the strategic objectives and goals of the organization. It helps leaders identify the need for change, define the desired outcomes, and develop a roadmap for implementation. By aligning change efforts with the organization's mission, vision, and values, change management ensures that initiatives contribute to long-term success and sustainability.

Driving Innovation and Adaptability: Change management fosters a culture of innovation and adaptability within organizations. It encourages employees to embrace new ideas, challenge the status quo, and seek continuous improvement. By embedding change as a core competency, organizations can respond effectively to market shifts, seize opportunities, and remain competitive in a rapidly changing business landscape.

Change management is not just a buzzword; it is a critical discipline for organizations that want to thrive in today's dynamic world. By recognizing the importance of change management, organizations can navigate transitions more effectively, minimize resistance, maximize adoption, enhance employee engagement, align objectives, and drive innovation. Change management is not a one-time event but an ongoing process that requires proactive leadership, effective communication, and the support of all stakeholders. Investing in change management capabilities is an investment in the long-term success and resilience of organizations in an ever-changing business environment.

CHAPTER 2

THE POWER OF HABIT STACKING IN DRIVING SUCCESSFUL CHANGE

Change is often met with resistance and can be challenging to implement within organizations. However, by leveraging the power of habit stacking, organizations can overcome these hurdles and drive successful change. This chapter explores the concept of habit stacking and its transformative impact on organizational change efforts.

Understanding Habit Stacking

Habit stacking is a strategy rooted in the understanding that lasting change is best achieved by building upon existing habits and routines. It involves consciously linking new actions or behaviors to established ones, creating a chain of habits that facilitate the adoption of desired changes. By leveraging the power of habit stacking, organizations can tap into existing routines and seamlessly integrate new behaviors, processes, and mindsets.

The Science Behind Habit Stacking

Habit stacking is grounded in the science of habit formation and behavior change. Our brains are wired to seek efficiency and conserve energy, leading to the formation of habitual behaviors. When we repeat behaviors in a consistent context, they become automatic and require less cognitive effort. Habit stacking capitalizes on this natural inclination, utilizing existing habits as anchors for introducing new behaviors.

The Power of Association

Habit stacking works by associating a new behavior with an existing, well-established habit. By linking the new behavior to a pre-existing cue or trigger, organizations can tap into the neural pathways that support habit formation. This association allows the new behavior to piggyback on the existing habit, making it easier to adopt and sustain over time.

Seamless Integration of Change

Habit stacking facilitates the seamless integration of change within organizations. By identifying the critical behaviors that need to change and mapping them onto existing habits, organizations can create a smooth transition process. For example, if the goal is to improve communication within teams, habit stacking can link the new behavior of regular team meetings to an existing habit, such as the daily coffee break. This integration makes the adoption of the new behavior feel natural and effortless.

Enhancing Adoption and Sustainability

One of the key advantages of habit stacking is its ability to enhance the adoption and sustainability of change. When new behaviors are linked to existing habits, they become part of employees' routines, making them more likely to be adopted and maintained over time. This integration also increases the chances of the new behaviors becoming automatic, reducing the cognitive load and effort required to sustain them.

Cultivating a Culture of Change

Habit stacking is not only a strategy for individual behavior change but also a catalyst for organizational culture change. By embedding desired behaviors through habit stacking, organizations can cultivate a culture that embraces change and continuous improvement. When habit stacking becomes a shared practice, it fosters an environment where change is embraced as a natural part of operations, rather than being met with resistance.

Habit stacking harnesses the power of existing habits to drive successful change within organizations. By strategically linking new behaviors to established routines, organizations can overcome resistance, seamlessly integrate change, enhance adoption, and cultivate a culture of continuous improvement. Understanding the science behind habit formation and leveraging the power of association allows organizations to tap into the innate human inclination towards habits and make change a more effortless and sustainable process. By embracing habit stacking, organizations can unlock the potential for transformative change and position themselves for long-term success in a rapidly evolving business landscape.

CHAPTER 3

OVERVIEW OF THE BOOK'S CONTENT AND OBJECTIVES

This chapter provides an overview of the content and objectives of this book on change management and habit stacking. It outlines the key themes, case studies, and practical tools that will be explored throughout the book, highlighting how readers can benefit from the insights and strategies presented.

Exploring Change Management and Habit Stacking

The book aims to delve into two interconnected topics: change management and habit stacking. It begins by emphasizing the importance of change management in organizations, recognizing that change is a constant in today's business landscape. The chapter on change management explores the principles, strategies, and challenges involved in successfully managing organizational change. It highlights the impact of change management on minimizing resistance, maximizing adoption, enhancing employee engagement, and driving innovation.

Next, the book transitions to the concept of habit stacking and its transformative potential in driving successful change. It delves into the science behind habit formation and behavior change, explaining how habit stacking leverages existing routines to introduce and integrate new behaviors seamlessly. The chapter on habit stacking explores the power of association, the seamless integration of change, and the enhanced adoption and sustainability that result from this approach. It emphasizes the role of habit stacking in cultivating a culture of change within organizations.

Real-Life Case Studies

To illustrate the practical application of habit stacking, the book presents real-life case studies of organizations that have successfully utilized habit stacking to drive meaningful change. These case studies offer tangible examples of how habit stacking can be employed in various contexts, such as implementing new systems, transforming processes, or streamlining operations. Each case study showcases the challenges faced, the strategies employed, and the outcomes achieved through habit stacking. Readers can gain valuable insights and inspiration from these real-world examples, discovering how habit stacking can be tailored to their specific organizational needs.

Practical Tools and Frameworks

In addition to the theoretical discussions and case studies, the book provides readers with practical tools and frameworks to help them navigate the complexities of change management and harness the power of habit stacking within their organizations. These tools and frameworks are designed to assist leaders in implementing change initiatives, identifying critical behaviors for change, mapping existing habits, integrating new behaviors through habit stacking, and communicating and reinforcing change effectively. By offering practical guidance, the book enables readers to apply the concepts and strategies in their own organizational contexts.

Objectives

The primary objective of this book is to equip leaders, managers, and change agents with the knowledge, insights, and practical tools necessary to drive successful change within their organizations. It aims to empower readers to overcome resistance, foster adoption, enhance employee engagement, align change initiatives with organizational goals, and cultivate a culture of continuous improvement. By exploring the principles and strategies of change management and habit stacking, the book provides a comprehensive guide for driving meaningful organizational change.

The content and objectives of this book revolve around the vital topics of change management and habit stacking. Through theoretical discussions, real-life case studies, and practical tools, readers will gain a deeper understanding of how change can be effectively managed and how habit stacking can drive successful change initiatives. By embracing the insights and strategies presented, readers will be well-equipped to navigate the complexities of change, harness the power of habit stacking, and lead their organizations towards a more adaptable, innovative, and successful future.

CHAPTER 4

UNDERSTANDING CHANGE MANAGEMENT

Change is an inevitable and constant force in the business world. Organizations must adapt to internal and external factors to remain competitive and thrive in a rapidly evolving environment. However, managing change effectively is a complex task that requires a deep understanding of the principles and processes of change management. This chapter explores the foundational concepts and components of change management, providing readers with a comprehensive understanding of this critical discipline.

Defining Change Management

Change management refers to the structured approach and set of processes used to guide individuals, teams, and entire organizations through a planned transition from the current state to a desired future state. It involves identifying the need for change, developing a vision for the future, and implementing strategies to support individuals and teams in navigating the transition. Change management focuses on both the human and organizational aspects of change, ensuring that people are engaged, equipped, and empowered to embrace and drive the desired changes.

The Principles of Change Management

Clear Communication: Effective change management relies on clear and transparent communication. Leaders must articulate the reasons for change, the expected outcomes, and the impact on individuals and the organization. Transparent communication fosters understanding, reduces uncertainty, and minimizes resistance among employees.

Stakeholder Engagement: Change affects various stakeholders within an organization. Engaging key stakeholders, including employees, managers, and leaders, throughout the change process is crucial for successful implementation. By involving stakeholders early on and addressing their concerns and feedback, change management can gain support and ensure a smoother transition.

Leadership Support: Leadership plays a vital role in change management.

Leaders must demonstrate their commitment to change, provide guidance, and act as role models for desired behaviors. Effective leadership support inspires trust, motivates employees, and encourages them to embrace the change.

Training and Development: Change often requires employees to learn new skills, adopt new behaviors, and adapt to new processes. Providing adequate training and development opportunities ensures that employees are equipped to navigate the change successfully. Training programs should be designed to address specific needs and empower employees to embrace the new ways of working.

Change Readiness: Assessing the organization's readiness for change is crucial. Understanding the organization's culture, capabilities, and capacity to handle change helps identify potential barriers and opportunities. Change readiness assessments enable leaders to plan and tailor change strategies accordingly.

Navigating the Change Process

Change management follows a systematic process that guides organizations through the transition. This typically includes the following steps:

Identify the Need for Change: Recognize the triggers or catalysts that necessitate change, whether they are external market forces, internal inefficiencies, or emerging opportunities.

Develop a Vision: Create a compelling vision that communicates the desired future state and the benefits that will result from the change. The vision should inspire and engage employees, providing a clear direction for the change efforts.

Plan and Strategize: Develop a comprehensive change management plan that outlines the goals, objectives, strategies, and resources required to achieve the desired change. This plan should consider potential risks, mitigation strategies, and key milestones.

Implement and Monitor: Execute the change plan, ensuring that the necessary resources, training, and support are provided to employees. Regularly monitor progress, evaluate the effectiveness of interventions, and adjust as needed.

Sustain and Embed Change: Successful change management goes beyond the initial implementation phase. It involves embedding the change within the organization's culture, processes, and systems. This includes reinforcing new behaviors, providing ongoing support, and continuously monitoring and adapting to ensure the change is sustained.

Understanding change management is crucial for organizations seeking to thrive in an ever-changing business landscape. By grasping the principles, processes, and components of change management, leaders can effectively navigate the complexities of change, minimize resistance, and empower employees to embrace and drive successful change initiatives. With a solid foundation in change management, organizations can adapt, innovate, and remain competitive in the face of constant evolution.

CHAPTER 5

DEFINING CHANGE MANAGEMENT AND ITS PRINCIPLES

Change is an inherent part of the business landscape, and organizations must adapt to stay competitive and relevant. However, managing change effectively requires a structured and strategic approach. This chapter delves into the definition of change management and explores its principles, providing readers with a comprehensive understanding of this critical discipline.

Defining Change Management

Change management is the discipline and process of guiding individuals, teams, and organizations through a planned transition from the current state to a desired future state. It involves a systematic approach to understand, prepare for, and implement change initiatives within an organization. Change management aims to minimize disruption, mitigate resistance, and ensure that individuals and teams are equipped to embrace and drive the desired changes.

Principles of Change Management

Clear Objectives and Vision: Change management requires a clear understanding of the objectives and vision driving the change. It is essential to articulate the purpose and desired outcomes of the change initiative, providing a compelling vision that inspires and guides individuals and teams.

Stakeholder Engagement: Engaging stakeholders at all levels of the organization is crucial for successful change management. Stakeholders include employees, managers, leaders, and external partners who may be affected by or contribute to the change process. By involving stakeholders from the beginning, addressing their concerns, and seeking their input, change management can build support and minimize resistance.

Effective Communication: Communication is a cornerstone of change management. Clear and consistent communication helps employees understand the reasons for change, the impact on their roles, and the benefits that will result. Communication should be timely, transparent, and tailored to different audiences, ensuring that information is shared effectively and feedback is sought and addressed.

Empowering Leadership: Leadership plays a pivotal role in change management. Leaders must provide direction, support, and inspiration to guide individuals and teams through the change process. Effective leadership empowers employees, fosters trust, and motivates them to embrace the change and drive its successful implementation.

Resource Allocation and Planning: Adequate resources, including finances, time, and human capital, are critical for successful change management. Planning and allocating resources ensure that the necessary tools, training, and support are available to individuals and teams. Resource planning should consider potential risks, contingencies, and the capacity to handle the change effectively.

Continuous Learning and Adaptation: Change management is an iterative process that requires continuous learning and adaptation. It is essential to monitor progress, evaluate the effectiveness of interventions, and adjust as needed. A culture of learning and adaptability enables organizations to respond to emerging challenges and capitalize on new opportunities.

Sustainability and Embedding Change: Successful change management extends beyond the implementation phase. It involves embedding the change within the organizational culture, processes, and systems. Sustainability requires reinforcing new behaviors, providing ongoing support, and integrating the change into daily operations. By embedding change, organizations ensure long-term success and enable future transformation.

Change management is a vital discipline for organizations navigating the ever-changing business landscape. By defining change management and understanding its principles, leaders can effectively guide individuals and teams through planned transitions. Clear objectives, stakeholder engagement, effective communication, empowering leadership, resource planning, continuous learning, and sustainability are key principles that drive successful change management. By embracing these principles, organizations can minimize resistance, optimize outcomes, and create a culture of adaptability, ensuring their long-term success in a dynamic and evolving environment.

CHAPTER 6

THE PSYCHOLOGY OF CHANGE: WHY PEOPLE RESIST AND HOW TO OVERCOME RESISTANCE

Change can be a challenging and disruptive process for individuals and organizations alike. Understanding the psychology behind why people resist change is crucial for effective change management. This chapter explores the reasons behind resistance to change and provides strategies to overcome resistance, empowering individuals, and organizations to navigate change successfully.

Understanding Resistance to Change

Fear of the Unknown: Change often introduces uncertainty, and the unknown can be intimidating. People may resist change because they fear the potential risks, loss of familiarity, or the need to learn new skills. The fear of the unknown triggers an instinct to cling to what is known and comfortable.

Loss of Control: Change can disrupt individuals' sense of control over their work environment and processes. When people feel that change is imposed upon them without their involvement or input, they may resist out of a desire to maintain a sense of autonomy and control.

Disrupted Social Dynamics: Change can alter established social dynamics within teams or organizations. People may resist change if they fear it will disrupt relationships, challenge established power structures, or create uncertainty in their interpersonal interactions.

Attachment to the Status Quo: People often become attached to familiar routines, processes, and ways of doing things. The status quo provides a sense of stability and comfort, and change threatens to disrupt these established patterns. This attachment to the status quo can lead to resistance to change.

Perceived Loss of Benefits: Individuals may resist change if they perceive it as a potential loss of personal or professional benefits. They may fear that change will negatively impact their job security, compensation, or opportunities for growth. Resistance can be a protective mechanism to safeguard perceived benefits.

Overcoming Resistance to Change

Effective Communication: Clear and transparent communication is crucial for overcoming resistance. Leaders should communicate the reasons for change, the benefits it will bring, and address concerns and questions. By providing open channels of communication and involving employees in the change process, resistance can be minimized.

Empathy and Engagement: Leaders should empathize with employees' concerns and engage them in the change process. Involving individuals in decision-making, seeking their input, and valuing their perspectives helps create a sense of ownership and reduces resistance. Engaged employees are more likely to embrace change and become advocates for its success.

Education and Training: Providing education and training programs equips individuals with the necessary skills and knowledge to adapt to change. By offering opportunities for learning and development, organizations empower employees to navigate change effectively, reducing resistance stemming from fear of the unknown.

Addressing Losses and Concerns: Acknowledging and addressing the perceived losses and concerns associated with change is crucial. Leaders should provide support, reassurance, and guidance to help individuals manage the emotional impact of change. By addressing the root causes of resistance and providing solutions, leaders can help employees transition more smoothly.

Leading by Example: Leaders play a pivotal role in overcoming resistance to change. By demonstrating a positive attitude, embracing change themselves, and serving as role models, leaders inspire confidence and motivate others to do the same. Leading by example fosters a culture of openness and adaptability, helping overcome resistance.

Celebrating Success and Small Wins: Acknowledging and celebrating the milestones and successes achieved throughout the change process boosts morale and motivation. Recognizing individuals and teams for their efforts and accomplishments reinforces the benefits of change and encourages continued support and participation.

Understanding the psychology of change and why people resist is crucial for effective change management. By addressing the underlying fears, concerns, and attachments associated with change, organizations can implement strategies to overcome resistance. Through effective communication, empathy, education, addressing losses and concerns, leading by example, and celebrating successes, leaders can foster a culture that embraces change and empowers individuals to adapt, innovate, and thrive in an ever-evolving environment. Overcoming resistance paves the way for successful change implementation and enables organizations to achieve their desired outcomes.

CHAPTER 7

THE ROLE OF LEADERSHIP IN DRIVING AND SUPPORTING CHANGE

Leadership plays a pivotal role in driving and supporting change within organizations. Effective leadership is essential for successfully navigating the complexities of change, engaging employees, and ensuring the organization's long-term success. This chapter explores the critical role of leadership in change management, highlighting the key responsibilities and strategies that leaders can employ to drive and support change.

Setting the Vision and Direction

Leadership begins with setting a clear vision and direction for change. Effective leaders articulate the need for change, communicate a compelling vision of the desired future state, and define the strategic objectives and goals that will drive the change effort. By providing a clear direction, leaders inspire and motivate employees, aligning their efforts toward the desired outcomes.

Creating a Sense of Urgency

Leadership involves creating a sense of urgency that drives the change process forward. Effective leaders convey the importance and relevance of the change, highlighting the risks of inaction and the opportunities that change presents. By instilling a sense of urgency, leaders help overcome resistance and facilitate buy-in from employees, ensuring a collective commitment to change.

Building a Change-Oriented Culture

Leadership plays a crucial role in shaping and fostering a change-oriented culture within the organization. This involves creating an environment where innovation, adaptability, and continuous improvement are encouraged and rewarded. By modeling and promoting a culture that embraces change, leaders inspire employees to be open-minded, proactive, and willing to challenge the status quo.

Engaging and Communicating with Stakeholders

Leaders must actively engage and communicate with stakeholders throughout the change process. This involves listening to their concerns, addressing their questions, and involving them in decision-making. Effective communication helps build trust, reduces resistance, and creates a shared understanding of the change objectives and progress. Leaders must communicate transparently, authentically, and consistently to ensure that employees feel informed and included.

Empowering and Supporting Employees

Leadership entails empowering and supporting employees to embrace and drive change. Leaders should provide the necessary resources, training, and tools to help employees navigate the change effectively. This includes facilitating opportunities for learning and development, recognizing, and celebrating milestones, and addressing concerns or obstacles that arise along the way. By empowering employees, leaders foster a sense of ownership, commitment, and resilience in the face of change.

Leading by Example

Leadership is about leading by example. Leaders must embody the desired behaviors, attitudes, and values associated with the change. By modeling the desired behaviors, leaders inspire and motivate employees to follow suit. Authentic leadership builds trust, credibility, and confidence in the change process, enabling employees to see firsthand the benefits of embracing change.

Managing Resistance and Overcoming Obstacles

Leadership involves managing resistance to change and overcoming obstacles that arise during the change process. Effective leaders anticipate and address resistance, proactively addressing concerns, and seeking solutions to mitigate barriers to change. By actively listening, providing support, and fostering collaboration, leaders can create an environment where resistance is minimized, and obstacles are overcome.

Evaluating and Celebrating Success

Leadership includes evaluating the progress and impact of change initiatives. Leaders must establish metrics and measures to assess the effectiveness of the change efforts, identifying areas of success and areas for improvement. Celebrating successes, no matter how small, helps sustain motivation and momentum. Recognizing and rewarding individuals and teams for their contributions reinforces the value of change and encourages ongoing commitment to the desired outcomes.

Leadership is a critical driver of change within organizations. Effective leaders set a clear vision, create a sense of urgency, foster a change-oriented culture, engage stakeholders, empower employees, lead by example, manage resistance, and evaluate progress. By assuming these responsibilities, leaders provide the necessary guidance, support, and motivation to drive and support successful change efforts. With strong leadership, organizations can navigate change with confidence, adapt to new challenges, and position themselves for long-term success in a dynamic and evolving business landscape.

CHAPTER 8

CREATING A COMPELLING VISION FOR CHANGE

A compelling vision is a cornerstone of successful change management. It provides a clear direction, motivates employees, and guides the change process. This chapter explores the importance of creating a compelling vision for change and offers strategies to develop and communicate a vision that inspires and mobilizes individuals and teams towards desired outcomes.

The Power of a Compelling Vision

A compelling vision serves as a guiding light that illuminates the path forward during times of change. It articulates a clear picture of the desired future state, highlighting the benefits and opportunities that the change will bring. A compelling vision captivates the hearts and minds of employees, generating excitement, buy-in, and a shared sense of purpose.

Key Elements of a Compelling Vision

Clarity: A compelling vision must be clear and easily understandable. It should communicate the intended outcomes, objectives, and the overall direction of the change initiative. Clarity eliminates ambiguity and ensures that employees have a clear understanding of the vision and its implications.

Alignment with Values and Purpose: The vision should be aligned with the organization's core values and purpose. It should reflect the organization's identity and resonate with employees' sense of meaning and contribution. When the vision aligns with the organization's values, it fosters a sense of authenticity and inspires greater commitment.

Inspiration and Aspiration: A compelling vision should inspire and evoke a sense of aspiration. It should create excitement and motivate employees to strive for the future state. By painting a vivid picture of what success looks like, the vision fuels enthusiasm and drives individuals and teams to go above and beyond.

Strategies for Creating a Compelling Vision

Engage Stakeholders: Engaging stakeholders throughout the organization is essential for creating a compelling vision. Involve key stakeholders, including employees, managers, and leaders, in the visioning process. Seek their input, listen to their perspectives, and incorporate their ideas. Engaging stakeholders fosters a sense of ownership and ensures that the vision is inclusive and representative of the organization's diverse perspectives.

Communicate the Why: Clearly communicate the rationale behind the change and the reasons for the vision. Employees need to understand the compelling reasons for embarking on the change journey. Connect the vision to the organization's goals, market trends, and the needs of customers and stakeholders. By explaining the why, leaders build a solid foundation of understanding and support for the vision.

Paint a Vivid Picture: Use storytelling techniques to paint a vivid and inspiring picture of the future state. Create a narrative that describes the envisioned outcomes, benefits, and the positive impact on employees, customers, and the organization. By appealing to emotions and imagination, leaders can create an emotional connection and ignite enthusiasm for the vision.

Link to Individual and Team Contributions: Connect the vision to the contributions and impact of individuals and teams. Demonstrate how each person's efforts align with and contribute to the larger vision. By highlighting the importance of each person's role, leaders foster a sense of significance, purpose, and ownership, driving engagement and commitment.

Provide a Roadmap: Develop a roadmap that outlines the strategic objectives, milestones, and key initiatives required to achieve the vision. The roadmap provides a clear plan of action, instills confidence, and helps employees understand how their day-to-day efforts contribute to the overall vision. It also creates a sense of progress and momentum.

Reinforce and Repeat: Consistently reinforce the vision and its connection to the change initiatives. Communicate the vision through various channels, such as town hall meetings, newsletters, and team huddles. Repeat key messages to ensure that the vision remains at the forefront of employees' minds and remains a guiding force throughout the change process.

Creating a compelling vision for change is a critical step in successful change management. A well-crafted vision inspires, motivates, and provides a clear direction for individuals and teams. By engaging stakeholders, communicating the why, painting a vivid picture, linking to individual contributions, providing a roadmap, and reinforcing the vision, leaders can develop a compelling vision that guides the change effort. A compelling vision serves as a unifying force, rallying employees around a shared purpose and driving them towards the desired future state.

CHAPTER 9

THE CONCEPT OF HABIT STACKING

Habits are powerful drivers of human behavior, often operating on autopilot without conscious thought. The concept of habit stacking takes advantage of this natural inclination by leveraging existing habits to introduce and reinforce new behaviors. This chapter explores the concept of habit stacking, its underlying principles, and how it can be employed to drive positive change and achieve desired outcomes.

Understanding Habit Stacking

Habit stacking is a strategy that involves linking a new behavior to an existing habit, creating a chain of habits that facilitate the adoption of desired changes. It builds upon the foundation of existing routines, making it easier to integrate and sustain new behaviors. By capitalizing on the brain's neural pathways associated with habitual actions, habit stacking taps into the power of automaticity and leverages it to drive positive change.

The Power of Association

Habit stacking works on the principle of association. Our brains naturally link one behavior to another when they occur in a consistent sequence. By deliberately pairing a new behavior with an established habit, we take advantage of this natural association to make the new behavior more automatic and effortless. The existing habit serves as a trigger or cue for the new behavior, helping to solidify the connection and make the new behavior easier to adopt.

Seamless Integration of New Behaviors

Habit stacking enables the seamless integration of new behaviors into our daily routines. By selecting a specific time, place, or action as a trigger for the new behavior, we create a clear cue that signals the desired action. This integration makes the new behavior feel natural and effortless, reducing the cognitive load and willpower required to initiate and sustain the change. Over time, the new behavior becomes ingrained and automatic, seamlessly woven into our existing habits.

Selecting the Right Cues and Behaviors

Effective habit stacking requires careful selection of cues and behaviors. The cue should be closely related to the existing habit, making it easily recognizable and triggering the desired behavior. The new behavior should be small and achievable, ensuring that it is manageable and doesn't overwhelm individuals. Starting with small changes builds momentum and increases the likelihood of success, creating a positive feedback loop that encourages further change.

Examples of Habit Stacking

Habit stacking can be applied to various areas of life, including personal habits, professional routines, and organizational processes. For example, if the goal is to incorporate regular exercise into a daily routine, one could stack it with an existing habit like brushing teeth. The act of brushing teeth becomes the trigger to immediately engage in a short exercise routine. Over time, this habit stack reinforces the desired exercise behavior and makes it a natural part of the daily routine.

Benefits of Habit Stacking

Habit stacking offers several benefits for driving positive change:

Ease of Adoption: By leveraging existing habits, habit stacking makes it easier to adopt new behaviors. It minimizes the resistance and effort typically associated with behavior change, increasing the likelihood of successful adoption.

Sustainability: Habit stacking promotes sustainable change by embedding new behaviors within existing routines. The integration of the new behavior into daily life makes it more likely to be maintained over the long term.

Efficiency: Habit stacking capitalizes on existing habits, saving time and cognitive resources. By piggybacking on established routines, individuals can efficiently incorporate new behaviors without needing to start from scratch.

Building Momentum: Habit stacking allows individuals to build momentum by starting with small, achievable changes. Success in adopting one habit stack can motivate individuals to take on additional habit stacks, creating a positive cycle of change and growth.

The concept of habit stacking harnesses the power of existing habits to drive positive change. By leveraging the brain's natural inclination for associating behaviors, habit stacking makes it easier to adopt and sustain new behaviors. With careful selection of cues and behaviors, habit stacking enables the seamless integration of change into daily routines. Its benefits, including ease of adoption, sustainability, efficiency, and momentum building, make habit stacking a powerful tool for driving personal, professional, and organizational change. By understanding and employing the principles of habit stacking, individuals and organizations can transform their habits and achieve their desired outcomes more effectively.

CHAPTER 10

DEFINING HABIT STACKING AND ITS UNDERLYING PRINCIPLES

Habit stacking is a powerful strategy that leverages existing habits to introduce and reinforce new behaviors. It taps into the brain's natural inclination for automaticity and association, making behavior change easier and more sustainable. This chapter defines habit stacking and explores its underlying principles, shedding light on how it can be employed to drive positive change and facilitate personal and professional growth.

Defining Habit Stacking

Habit stacking is a technique that involves linking a new behavior, called the "target behavior," to an existing habit, called the "anchor habit." The anchor habit serves as a cue or trigger for the target behavior, making it more automatic and integrated into our daily routines. By stacking the target behavior onto an existing habit, we take advantage of the brain's neural pathways associated with habitual actions and create a chain of habits that facilitate change.

The Underlying Principles of Habit Stacking

The Power of Association: Habit stacking is based on the principle of association. When two behaviors occur in a consistent sequence, our brains naturally link them together. By deliberately pairing the target behavior with an established anchor habit, we take advantage of this natural association to make the new behavior more automatic and effortless. The anchor habit acts as a cue that triggers the target behavior, strengthening the connection between the two.

Leveraging Existing Habits: Habit stacking capitalizes on existing habits as a foundation for change. We all have established routines and habits that we perform on autopilot. By building upon these existing habits, we tap into the neural pathways that support habit formation. This leverage allows us to integrate new behaviors seamlessly into our daily lives, reducing resistance and making change more manageable.

Cue-Response-Reward Loop: Habit stacking operates within the framework of the cue-response-reward loop, which is fundamental to habit formation. The anchor habit serves as the cue, triggering the target behavior as the response.

When the target behavior is performed, it is followed by a reward, which reinforces the habit loop. By identifying the cue and ensuring a satisfying reward, habit stacking strengthens the loop and solidifies the new behavior.

Small, Achievable Changes: Habit stacking emphasizes starting with small, achievable changes. Breaking down the target behavior into manageable steps increases the likelihood of success and minimizes overwhelm. By focusing on one specific behavior at a time, individuals can build momentum and experience early wins, which fuel motivation and further habit formation.

Contextual Fit: Habit stacking requires selecting an anchor habit that is closely related or contextually fit with the target behavior. The anchor habit should naturally precede or occur near the target behavior. This contextual fit enhances the association between the two habits and ensures that the anchor habit effectively cues the target behavior.

Applying Habit Stacking

Habit stacking can be applied to various areas of life, such as personal habits, professional routines, or organizational processes. For example, if the goal is to develop a reading habit, an anchor habit like having a cup of tea in the evening can serve as the cue for reading. Each time the individual prepares a cup of tea, it triggers the behavior of sitting down with a book. Over time, this habit stack strengthens, making reading a natural part of the evening routine.

Benefits of Habit Stacking

Habit stacking offers several benefits for behavior change:

Simplified Change Process: By building on existing habits, habit stacking simplifies the change process. It taps into the brain's natural inclination for automaticity, making behavior change feel more effortless and manageable.

Increased Consistency: Habit stacking enhances consistency by linking the target behavior to a daily habit. This consistent repetition strengthens the habit loop and reinforces the new behavior, making it more likely to be performed consistently over time.

Time and Energy Efficiency: Leveraging existing habits allows individuals to make the most of their time and energy. By integrating new behaviors into established routines, individuals can achieve their goals without needing to allocate additional time and effort.

Enhanced Sustainability: Habit stacking promotes sustainable change by embedding new behaviors within existing habits. The integration of the target behavior into daily life makes it more likely to be maintained over the long term, reducing the risk of relapse.

Habit stacking is a powerful strategy for driving positive change and facilitating personal and professional growth. By leveraging the brain's natural inclination for association and automaticity, habit stacking makes behavior change easier and more sustainable. The underlying principles of association, leveraging existing habits, cue-response-reward loops, small achievable changes, and contextual fit contribute to the effectiveness of habit stacking. By understanding and applying these principles, individuals can harness the power of habit stacking to create lasting change and achieve their desired outcomes.

CHAPTER 11

HOW HABIT STACKING LEVERAGES EXISTING ROUTINES FOR SUCCESSFUL CHANGE

Habit stacking is a powerful technique that leverages existing routines to facilitate successful change. By building new behaviors upon established habits, habit stacking taps into the brain's neural pathways, making change more automatic and sustainable. This chapter explores how habit stacking leverages existing routines and outlines the benefits of this approach for driving successful change.

Understanding Habit Stacking

Habit stacking involves linking a new behavior, known as the "target behavior," to an existing habit, called the "anchor habit." The anchor habit serves as a cue or trigger for the target behavior, allowing the new behavior to piggyback on the existing routine. By leveraging the brain's natural inclination for automaticity and association, habit stacking helps integrate the target behavior seamlessly into daily life.

Leveraging the Power of Automaticity

The human brain is wired to automate repetitive behaviors, conserving mental energy, and making actions more efficient. Habit stacking leverages this innate ability by connecting the target behavior to an established routine. The brain recognizes the familiar anchor habit as a cue and automatically triggers the subsequent target behavior, making it easier to adopt and sustain the desired change.

Creating a Chain of Habits

Habit stacking creates a chain of habits that reinforces the target behavior. By consistently associating the target behavior with the anchor habit, individuals strengthen the neural pathways associated with the new behavior. Over time, the chain of habits becomes stronger, and the target behavior becomes ingrained in the daily routine.

Minimizing Resistance to Change

Resistance to change often stems from the disruption of established routines and the perceived effort required to adopt new behaviors. Habit stacking addresses these challenges by minimizing resistance. By integrating the target behavior into an existing routine, individuals experience less cognitive load and resistance, as the change feels like a natural extension of their everyday activities.

Identifying Anchor Habits

To leverage existing routines effectively, it is crucial to identify suitable anchor habits. An anchor habit should be a behavior that is consistently performed and is closely related to the desired target behavior. The anchor habit should act as a reliable trigger or cue for the target behavior, making the association between the two habits clear and easily recognizable.

Seamless Integration of New Behaviors

Habit stacking enables the seamless integration of new behaviors into existing routines. By selecting the right anchor habit, individuals ensure that the target behavior fits naturally within the context of their daily activities. This integration reduces the cognitive effort required to initiate and sustain the new behavior, increasing the likelihood of successful change adoption.

Examples of Habit Stacking

Habit stacking can be applied to various aspects of life, such as personal habits, professional routines, or organizational processes. For instance, if the goal is to incorporate regular stretching into a daily routine, an anchor habit like brushing teeth in the morning can be used. After brushing teeth, the anchor habit triggers the target behavior of performing a few stretches. Over time, this habit stack becomes automatic and ingrained in the morning routine.

Benefits of Habit Stacking

Increased Adoption and Sustainability: By leveraging existing routines, habit stacking increases the likelihood of adopting new behaviors and sustaining them over the long term. The integration into established habits makes the change feel effortless and natural, leading to greater consistency and sustainability.

Efficient Use of Time and Energy: Habit stacking optimizes time and energy by capitalizing on existing routines. Individuals can incorporate new behaviors without needing to allocate additional time or effort, making change more feasible and sustainable in busy lifestyles.

Enhanced Consistency and Progress: The integration of the target behavior within existing routines promotes consistency and progress. By consistently performing the target behavior through habit stacking, individuals build momentum and experience a sense of accomplishment, reinforcing their commitment to the change process.

Reduction in Resistance: Habit stacking minimizes resistance to change by integrating new behaviors into established routines. Individuals are less likely to encounter the friction and discomfort often associated with adopting new habits, making change more seamless and enjoyable.

Habit stacking leverages the power of existing routines to facilitate successful change. By linking the target behavior to an anchor habit, individuals tap into the brain's natural inclination for automaticity and association. This approach minimizes resistance, optimizes time and energy, and promotes the adoption and sustainability of new behaviors. By understanding and applying the principles of habit stacking, individuals can leverage their existing routines to drive successful change and achieve their desired outcomes.

CHAPTER 12

THE SCIENCE BEHIND HABIT FORMATION AND BEHAVIOR CHANGE

Habits play a significant role in our daily lives, shaping our behaviors and routines. Understanding the science behind habit formation and behavior change is essential for effectively transforming our habits and achieving desired outcomes. This chapter delves into the science behind habit formation and behavior change, exploring the key concepts and mechanisms that drive our habits.

The Habit Loop

At the core of habit formation is the habit loop, a three-step process that involves a cue, a routine, and a reward. The cue serves as a trigger that initiates the habit, the routine represents the behavior itself, and the reward provides a sense of satisfaction or reinforcement. This loop is driven by the brain's automatic response to repeated cues, making habits more automatic and less reliant on conscious decision-making.

Neuroplasticity and Habit Formation

Neuroplasticity, the brain's ability to reorganize and form new neural connections, plays a crucial role in habit formation. When a behavior is consistently repeated, the associated neural pathways become stronger and more efficient. This rewiring of the brain enhances the automaticity of the behavior, making it easier to perform and reinforcing the habit loop.

The Role of Dopamine

Dopamine, a neurotransmitter associated with pleasure and reward, plays a significant role in habit formation. When we engage in a behavior that provides a pleasurable reward, such as eating a delicious meal or receiving positive feedback, dopamine is released, reinforcing the habit loop. The anticipation of the reward creates a craving for the behavior, further solidifying the habit.

Cue-Response-Reward Associations

Habit formation relies on the brain's ability to associate cues with specific behaviors and rewards. When a cue is consistently paired with a particular routine and followed by a satisfying reward, the brain establishes a strong association between the three components. Over time, the presence of the cue triggers an automatic response, leading to the performance of the routine and the expectation of the reward.

Habit Formation and the Basal Ganglia

The basal ganglia, a region of the brain responsible for procedural learning and habit formation, plays a critical role in habit formation. As habits become ingrained, the basal ganglia take over the automatic execution of behaviors, freeing up cognitive resources for other tasks. This shift from conscious effort to automaticity allows habits to be performed with less mental effort.

The Power of Context and Environmental Cues

Context and environmental cues have a significant impact on habit formation and behavior change. Our surroundings, such as our physical environment, social settings, or emotional states, can act as powerful triggers for specific habits. By manipulating the environment and introducing cues that prompt desired behaviors, we can shape and reinforce new habits.

Breaking and Rewiring Habits

Behavior change often involves breaking existing habits and replacing them with new ones. This process requires awareness of the cues that trigger unwanted behaviors and conscious effort to replace the routine with a new, desired behavior. By consistently practicing the new behavior and associating it with a rewarding outcome, we can rewire the neural pathways and establish new, healthier habits.

The Role of Willpower and Motivation

Willpower and motivation play a crucial role in habit formation and behavior change. While habits operate on automaticity, initially, conscious effort and self-control are required to establish new behaviors. As habits become more automatic, willpower is preserved, and the behavior requires less conscious effort. Motivation acts as the driving force that sustains our efforts in adopting new habits and overcoming challenges along the way.

Understanding the science behind habit formation and behavior change provides valuable insights into how we can effectively transform our habits. By leveraging the habit loop, neuroplasticity, dopamine, cue-response-reward associations, the basal ganglia, and the power of context, we can shape our behaviors and create lasting change. With conscious effort, awareness of environmental cues, and motivation, we can break unwanted habits, rewire our neural pathways, and establish new habits that align with our goals and desired outcomes. Applying the science of habit formation empowers us to make positive changes in our lives and pave the way for personal and professional growth.

CHAPTER 13

THE BENEFITS OF HABIT STACKING IN DRIVING SUSTAINABLE CHANGE

Habit stacking is a powerful strategy for driving sustainable change by leveraging existing routines and habits. By intentionally linking new behaviors to established habits, habit stacking creates a chain of habits that facilitates the adoption and maintenance of desired changes. This chapter explores the benefits of habit stacking in driving sustainable change and achieving long-term success.

Increased Adoption and Consistency

One of the key benefits of habit stacking is the increased adoption and consistency of new behaviors. By integrating the target behavior into an existing routine, individuals are more likely to adopt the behavior as it feels like a natural extension of their daily activities. The anchor habit serves as a cue or trigger, making it easier to initiate the desired behavior consistently. As the new behavior becomes ingrained in the routine, individuals are more likely to maintain consistency over time, leading to sustainable change.

Leveraging Existing Neural Pathways

Habit stacking takes advantage of the brain's natural inclination for automaticity and neural pathways. By building upon existing habits, the new behavior piggybacks on the neural pathways that have already been established. This leverage makes it easier for the brain to execute the new behavior, reducing the cognitive effort required. As the neural connections associated with the new behavior strengthen, it becomes more automatic, further reinforcing sustainable change.

Improved Efficiency and Time Management

Habit stacking optimizes efficiency and time management by leveraging existing routines. Instead of allocating additional time and effort to develop new habits, habit stacking integrates the desired behavior seamlessly into established activities. This integration ensures that individuals make the most of their existing time and routines, eliminating the need for extensive planning or dedicated practice sessions. By efficiently utilizing time, habit stacking promotes sustainable change without overburdening individuals' schedules.

Reduction of Decision Fatigue

Decision fatigue refers to the decline in decision-making quality and self-control that occurs after prolonged decision-making. Habit stacking helps reduce decision fatigue by automating behaviors and minimizing the need for active decision-making. Once the new behavior becomes a habit through habit stacking, individuals no longer need to make a conscious decision to engage in the behavior. This reduction in decision fatigue preserves mental energy, allowing individuals to focus on other important tasks and priorities.

Anchoring Behavior to Environmental Cues

Habit stacking capitalizes on environmental cues to reinforce the desired behavior. The anchor habit serves as a cue, triggering the target behavior in response to a specific context or situation. This association between the anchor habit and the target behavior helps individuals anchor the desired behavior to specific environmental cues, making it easier to perform the behavior consistently. Over time, individuals become more attuned to these cues, further solidifying the habit, and driving sustainable change.

Building Momentum and Self-Efficacy

Habit stacking allows individuals to build momentum and develop a sense of self-efficacy in the change process. Starting with small, achievable changes through habit stacking creates early wins, boosting confidence and motivation. As individuals successfully stack one habit upon another, they gain a sense of progress and achievement, reinforcing their belief in their ability to make lasting change. This positive momentum and increased self-efficacy contribute to the sustainability of behavior change efforts.

Adaptable and Scalable Approach

Habit stacking is an adaptable and scalable approach to driving sustainable change. It can be applied to various areas of life, from personal habits to professional routines or organizational processes. The flexibility of habit stacking allows individuals to start with small changes and gradually scale up, incorporating new habit stacks as desired behaviors become automatic. This adaptability ensures that individuals can continue to drive sustainable change and adapt their habits to evolving circumstances and goals.

Habit stacking offers numerous benefits in driving sustainable change. By leveraging existing routines and habits, habit stacking increases adoption, consistency, and efficiency in adopting new behaviors. It takes advantage of the brain's automaticity and neural pathways, reducing cognitive effort and decision fatigue. By anchoring behavior to environmental cues, habit stacking reinforces the desired behavior and promotes sustainability. Building momentum and self-efficacy, habit stacking empowers individuals to make lasting change and adapt their habits over time. With its adaptable and scalable nature, habit stacking provides a framework for driving sustainable change across various aspects of life. By harnessing the benefits of habit stacking, individuals can pave the way for long-term success in achieving their desired outcomes.

CHAPTER 14

REAL-LIFE CASE STUDIES: ORGANIZATIONS THAT UTILIZED HABIT STACKING

Habit stacking is a powerful technique that has been employed by organizations to drive meaningful change and foster sustainable habits among employees. This chapter explores real-life case studies of organizations that successfully utilized habit stacking as a strategy for achieving their goals and transforming their workplace culture. These case studies demonstrate the effectiveness of habit stacking in driving positive change at the organizational level.

Case Study 1

Finley Healthcare-Promoting Health and Wellness

Finley Healthcare, a large multinational corporation, aimed to promote health and wellness among its employees. They implemented habit stacking by leveraging existing routines and habits within the workplace. For instance, they introduced standing desks and encouraged employees to incorporate standing breaks during their workday. The anchor habit of standing was linked to routine activities such as checking emails or making phone calls. This habit stack not only encouraged physical activity but also improved posture and overall well-being. By seamlessly integrating the new behavior into existing work routines, Finley Healthcare successfully fostered a culture of health and wellness among its employees.

Case Study 2

Innovation Partners-Enhancing Collaboration

Innovation Partners, a non-profit organization, sought to enhance collaboration and communication among its teams. They employed habit stacking by utilizing existing routines and technology tools. For example, they established a habit stack of using collaborative online platforms for project management and document sharing. The anchor habit of accessing these platforms was linked to routine activities like team meetings or project updates. This habit stack facilitated seamless communication, streamlined workflows, and improved collaboration among team members. By integrating these new behaviors into existing routines and leveraging technology, Innovation

Partners successfully transformed its team dynamics and achieved greater efficiency and collaboration.

Case Study 3

Star Nexus, Inc.-Fostering a Culture of Learning

Star Nexus, Inc., a technology startup, prioritized a culture of continuous learning and development. They implemented habit stacking by incorporating learning opportunities into employees' daily routines. For instance, they encouraged employees to dedicate a specific time each day for reading or engaging in online courses. The anchor habit of setting aside learning time was linked to routine activities like lunch breaks or commuting. This habit stack fostered a culture of continuous learning, knowledge sharing, and personal growth within the organization. By leveraging existing routines and providing dedicated time for learning, Star Nexus successfully nurtured a culture of ongoing development and innovation.

Benefits and Lessons Learned

These real-life case studies highlight several benefits and lessons learned from utilizing habit stacking in organizations:

Seamless Integration: Habit stacking enables the seamless integration of new behaviors into existing routines. This integration reduces resistance and facilitates the adoption and sustainability of desired changes.

Employee Engagement: Habit stacking engages employees by leveraging their existing habits and routines. This approach empowers employees to take ownership of their habits and fosters a sense of personal investment in the change process.

Cultural Transformation: Habit stacking can drive cultural transformation within organizations. By linking desired behaviors to existing habits, organizations can shape their workplace culture and create new norms and expectations.

Incremental Change: Habit stacking allows for incremental change by starting with small, achievable habits. This approach builds momentum, increases self-efficacy, and paves the way for larger and more significant changes over time.

Measurement and Evaluation: Organizations that utilize habit stacking often monitor and evaluate the impact of the implemented habit stacks. By tracking progress and measuring outcomes, organizations can refine their approaches and ensure continuous improvement.

Real-life case studies of organizations that utilized habit stacking demonstrate the effectiveness of this strategy in driving positive change.

Whether it is promoting health and wellness, enhancing collaboration and communication, or fostering a culture of learning and development, habit stacking has proven to be a valuable tool for achieving organizational goals and transforming workplace culture. By leveraging existing routines and habits, organizations can seamlessly integrate new behaviors, engage employees, drive cultural transformation, and achieve sustainable change. These case studies highlight the power and potential of habit stacking as a strategy for driving meaningful change within organizations.

Case Study 4

ForkLab's-Implementation of a New System

ForkLab, a global technology company, recognized the need to revamp its performance management system to drive employee engagement and improve overall organizational performance. To accomplish this, they implemented a new performance management system using the strategy of habit stacking. This chapter explores the case study of ForkLab and how they successfully implemented the new performance management system through habit stacking.

Background

ForkLab had been using a traditional annual performance review process that was time-consuming, lacked real-time feedback, and failed to align individual goals with organizational objectives. The company identified the need for a more agile and collaborative approach to performance management. They aimed to foster continuous feedback, goal alignment, and personal development among employees.

Implementation Process

Defining the Target Behavior: The first step was to define the desired target behavior—regular and meaningful feedback and goal setting between managers and employees. The objective was to establish a culture of ongoing feedback and performance conversations.

Identifying the Anchor Habit: ForkLab identified an existing routine that could serve as an anchor habit to trigger the target behavior. They chose weekly team meetings, which already had a consistent schedule and were attended by managers and their respective teams.

Introducing the New Behavior: During the weekly team meetings, managers were encouraged to incorporate a dedicated feedback and goal-setting session. This session became the new behavior associated with the anchor habit of team meetings.

Training and Support: To facilitate the habit stack, ForkLab provided training and resources to managers on effective feedback techniques, goal setting, and the importance of ongoing performance conversations. This support helped managers understand the value of the new behavior and feel confident in their ability to implement it.

Monitoring and Evaluation: ForkLab implemented a system to monitor and evaluate the progress of the habit stack. They tracked the frequency and quality of feedback and goal-setting sessions conducted during team meetings. Regular check-ins and feedback loops allowed for continuous improvement and refinement of the habit stack.

Benefits and Results

The implementation of habit stacking for the new performance management system yielded several benefits for ForkLab:

Increased Employee Engagement: The habit stack encouraged regular and meaningful feedback, leading to increased employee engagement. Employees felt heard and supported, fostering a sense of empowerment and motivation.

Improved Goal Alignment: The new performance management system, enabled by habit stacking, facilitated goal alignment between individual employees and organizational objectives. Clear and aligned goals contributed to improved performance and increased overall productivity.

Continuous Learning and Development: The ongoing feedback and goal-setting sessions provided opportunities for continuous learning and development. Employees received timely insights and guidance for improvement, leading to enhanced skills and growth.

Enhanced Manager-Employee Relationships: Habit stacking improved the manager-employee relationship by fostering open communication and trust. Managers became more approachable, and employees felt comfortable sharing their concerns and aspirations.

Agility and Adaptability: The new performance management system, supported by habit stacking, allowed for agility and adaptability. It facilitated real-time feedback and course corrections, enabling employees to respond to changing circumstances and improve their performance promptly.

Lessons Learned

ForkLab's case study offers valuable lessons for successful implementation of habit stacking in performance management:

Clear Objectives: Defining clear objectives and target behaviors is crucial for successful habit stacking. Clearly articulating the desired behavior and outcomes ensures alignment throughout the organization.

Integration with Existing Routines: Identifying anchor habits that are already part of existing routines increases the chances of successful habit stacking. Integration with established routines makes the new behavior feel seamless and natural.

Training and Support: Providing adequate training and support to managers and employees is essential. It builds confidence, reinforces the importance of the new behavior, and ensures its successful implementation.

Regular Monitoring and Feedback: Regular monitoring and feedback loops allow for continuous improvement and adjustment of the habit stack. It provides insights into the effectiveness of the new behavior and allows for timely intervention if needed.

ForkLab's successful implementation of a new performance management system through habit stacking demonstrates the effectiveness of this approach. By leveraging existing routines and anchoring the desired behavior to team meetings, ForkLab fostered a culture of ongoing feedback and goal setting. The benefits of increased employee engagement, improved goal alignment, continuous learning and development, enhanced manager-employee relationships, and agility were realized through this habit stack. The lessons learned from this case study can guide other organizations in implementing habit stacking to drive successful performance management systems and create a positive and productive work environment.

Case Study 5

Norman Corporation's-Transformation of Processes

Norman Corporation, a leading retail company, embarked on a journey to transform its customer service processes to deliver exceptional customer experiences. To achieve this, they employed the strategy of habit stacking, linking new behaviors to existing routines within their customer service teams. This chapter explores the case study of ABC Corporation and how they successfully implemented habit stacking to drive significant improvements in their customer service processes.

Background

Norman Corporation recognized that their customer service processes needed to be more customer-centric, efficient, and personalized. They aimed to enhance response times, improve problem-solving abilities, and foster a customer-first culture within their customer service teams. To achieve these objectives, they turned to habit stacking as a strategy to drive sustainable change.

Implementation Process

Identifying Target Behaviors: The first step for Norman Corporation was to identify the specific target behaviors they wanted to cultivate within their customer service teams. These behaviors included active listening, empathetic communication, and effective problem-solving.

Analyzing Existing Routines: Norman Corporation analyzed the existing customer service processes and routines to identify anchor habits that could serve as triggers for the target behaviors. They discovered that routine activities like opening customer service tickets and reviewing customer history provided suitable anchor habits.

Linking Target Behaviors to Anchor Habits: Norman Corporation introduced new behaviors that were linked to the anchor habits. For example, when customer service representatives opened a customer service ticket, they were prompted to actively listen to the customer's concerns, demonstrate empathy, and proactively seek solutions.

Training and Skill Development: To ensure successful habit stacking, Norman Corporation provided comprehensive training and skill development programs to their customer service teams. They focused on enhancing active listening skills, empathetic communication, and problem-solving techniques.

Reinforcement and Recognition: Norman Corporation implemented a system to reinforce and recognize the desired behaviors. Managers provided positive feedback, acknowledged exemplary performance, and celebrated team achievements, fostering a culture that valued and reinforced the new behaviors.

Benefits and Results

The implementation of habit stacking within Norman Corporation's customer service processes resulted in several benefits:

Enhanced Customer Experience: Habit stacking improved the overall customer experience by promoting active listening, empathy, and effective problem-solving. Customers felt heard, valued, and experienced quicker resolutions to their concerns.

Improved Efficiency: The new behaviors linked to existing routines streamlined the customer service processes, resulting in improved efficiency. Customer service representatives were better equipped to handle customer issues promptly and provide satisfactory solutions.

Employee Empowerment: Habit stacking empowered customer service representatives to take ownership of customer interactions and find creative solutions. The link between anchor habits and target behaviors gave them a structured approach, increasing confidence and job satisfaction.

Positive Team Culture: Habit stacking fostered a positive team culture within the customer service department. The shared commitment to the target behaviors created a supportive and collaborative environment where team members encouraged and motivated each other.

Continuous Improvement: The habit stacking approach encouraged continuous improvement in customer service processes. Regular evaluation and feedback loops allowed for refinement of the new behaviors, addressing challenges, and adapting to evolving customer needs.

Lessons Learned

Norman Corporation's case study provides valuable lessons for implementing habit stacking in customer service processes:

Targeted Behavior Identification: Clearly identifying the desired target behaviors is crucial for successful habit stacking. Aligning these behaviors with customer service objectives ensures a customer-centric approach.

Anchor Habit Selection: Analyzing existing routines and selecting appropriate anchor habits improves the effectiveness of habit stacking. Choosing routines that naturally occur within the customer service processes enhances the integration of the new behaviors.

Skill Development and Training: Providing comprehensive training and skill development programs is essential for equipping employees with the necessary tools to adopt the new behaviors. Continuous training reinforces the target behaviors and ensures their successful implementation.

Reinforcement and Recognition: Establishing a system for reinforcing and recognizing the desired behaviors is vital for sustaining habit stacking efforts. Positive feedback and recognition motivate employees, foster a positive work culture, and reinforce the new behaviors.

Conclusion

Norman Corporation's successful transformation in customer service processes through habit stacking showcases the power of this strategy. By linking new behaviors to existing routines, Norman Corporation cultivated a customer-centric culture, improved efficiency, and empowered their customer service teams. The benefits of enhanced customer experiences, improved efficiency, employee empowerment, positive team culture, and continuous improvement were realized through habit stacking. The lessons learned from this case study provide valuable insights for organizations seeking to implement habit stacking in their customer service processes, driving meaningful and sustainable change.

Case Study 6

DEF-Adoption of Habit Stacking

DEF Non-profit, a community-based organization, recognized the need to streamline their volunteer management processes to enhance efficiency and maximize the impact of their programs. To achieve this, they implemented habit stacking as a strategy to create seamless and effective volunteer management routines. This chapter explores the case study of DEF Non-profit and how they successfully adopted habit stacking to streamline their volunteer management processes.

Background

DEF Non-profit relied heavily on volunteers to support their various programs and initiatives. However, their volunteer management processes were often time-consuming, inconsistent, and prone to errors. To address these challenges, DEF Non-profit sought a solution that would simplify and streamline their volunteer management efforts while maintaining a high level of volunteer engagement.

Implementation Process

Identifying Target Behaviors: DEF Non-profit identified specific target behaviors that were essential for effective volunteer management, including volunteer recruitment, onboarding, scheduling, and ongoing communication.

Analyzing Existing Routines: DEF Non-profit analyzed their existing volunteer management processes and routines to identify anchor habits that could serve as triggers for the target behaviors. They identified routine activities such as weekly volunteer team meetings and program planning sessions as suitable anchor habits.

Linking Target Behaviors to Anchor Habits: DEF Non-profit introduced new behaviors that were linked to the anchor habits. For example, during the weekly volunteer team meetings, a portion of the agenda was dedicated to volunteer recruitment and scheduling, ensuring these tasks were consistently addressed.

Standardizing Processes and Tools: To support habit stacking, DEF Non-profit standardized their volunteer management processes and implemented digital tools and platforms. This allowed for streamlined communication, volunteer sign-ups, and scheduling, reducing manual effort and improving efficiency.

Training and Support: DEF Non-profit provided training and support to their staff and volunteers to ensure successful habit stacking implementation. They conducted training sessions on the new processes, tools, and the importance of adhering to the target behaviors.

Continuous Evaluation and Improvement: DEF Non-profit established a feedback loop to continuously evaluate and improve the habit stack. Regular check-ins, volunteer surveys, and stakeholder feedback were utilized to identify areas for refinement and make necessary adjustments.

Benefits and Results

The implementation of habit stacking within DEF Non-profit's volunteer management processes resulted in several benefits:

Streamlined Processes: Habit stacking enabled DEF Non-profit to streamline their volunteer management processes. By linking target behaviors to anchor habits, they created a structured and consistent approach to volunteer recruitment, onboarding, scheduling, and communication.

Improved Efficiency: The standardized processes and digital tools facilitated efficient volunteer management. Volunteer recruitment and scheduling became quicker and more accurate, reducing administrative burden and enabling staff to focus on program execution and volunteer engagement.

Enhanced Volunteer Engagement: The habit stacking approach fostered better volunteer engagement. Volunteers experienced a more organized and streamlined experience, allowing them to contribute effectively and feel valued as part of the organization.

Clear Communication and Expectations: The adoption of habit stacking improved communication between staff and volunteers. The anchor habits ensured that important information, such as program updates and volunteer opportunities, was consistently shared during team meetings, enabling clear expectations, and reducing confusion.

Scalability and Replicability: The habit stacking approach allowed DEF Non-profit to scale their volunteer management efforts. The standardized processes and tools could be easily replicated across different programs and initiatives, ensuring consistency and efficiency throughout the organization.

Lessons Learned

DEF Non-profit's case study provides valuable lessons for other non-profit organizations seeking to streamline volunteer management through habit stacking:

Targeted Behavior Identification: Clearly identifying the target behaviors is essential for successful habit stacking. Understanding the specific needs and challenges of volunteer management enables organizations to focus on the behaviors that will have the most significant impact.

Anchor Habit Selection: Analyzing existing routines and selecting appropriate anchor habits ensures seamless integration of the new behaviors. Choosing routines that occur regularly and involve relevant stakeholders helps embed the target behaviors effectively.

Standardization and Technology: Standardizing processes and utilizing digital tools simplify volunteer management. Technology platforms can streamline communication, scheduling, and data management, enhancing efficiency and reducing manual effort.

Training and Support: Providing comprehensive training and ongoing support to staff and volunteers is crucial for successful habit stacking. Education on the new processes, tools, and the value of adhering to the target behaviors ensures a smooth transition and consistent implementation.

Continuous Improvement: Establishing a feedback loop allows for continuous evaluation and improvement of the habit stack. Regular feedback from volunteers and stakeholders helps identify areas for refinement and fine-tuning the volunteer management processes.

Conclusion

DEF Non-profit's successful adoption of habit stacking to streamline their volunteer management processes demonstrates the effectiveness of this approach. By linking target behaviors to existing routines, DEF Non-profit created a structured and efficient volunteer management system. The benefits of streamlined processes, improved efficiency, enhanced volunteer engagement, clear communication, and scalability were realized through habit stacking. The lessons learned from this case study provide valuable insights for non-profit organizations seeking to streamline their volunteer management efforts, ultimately maximizing their impact, and creating a positive volunteer experience.

CHAPTER 15

LESSONS LEARNED AND KEY TAKEAWAYS FROM CASE STUDIES

The case studies presented throughout this book have highlighted the successful implementation of habit stacking in various organizational contexts. Each case study has provided valuable insights into the benefits, challenges, and strategies involved in leveraging habit stacking for driving meaningful change. In this chapter, we will discuss the key lessons learned and key takeaways from the case studies, offering guidance for organizations looking to apply habit stacking in their own contexts.

Lesson 1: Clear Identification of Target Behaviors

A crucial lesson learned from the case studies is the importance of clearly identifying the target behaviors that align with organizational goals and desired outcomes. Defining the specific behaviors allows for a focused approach in implementing habit stacking. By clearly articulating the desired behaviors, organizations can ensure alignment throughout the organization and enhance the chances of success.

Lesson 2: Leveraging Existing Routines and Anchor Habits

The case studies have demonstrated the effectiveness of leveraging existing routines and anchor habits in implementing habit stacking. Integrating new behaviors into established routines makes the change feel seamless and natural. By selecting appropriate anchor habits, organizations can create strong associations that trigger the desired behaviors. This lesson emphasizes the need for careful analysis of existing routines to identify suitable anchor habits.

Lesson 3: Training, Support, and Skill Development

The successful implementation of habit stacking relies on providing adequate training, support, and skill development to individuals involved in the change process. The case studies have shown that organizations that invest in comprehensive training programs and ongoing support increase the likelihood of successful habit stacking. Equipping individuals with the necessary tools, knowledge, and skills helps them adopt and sustain the new behaviors effectively.

Lesson 4: Continuous Evaluation and Feedback

Continuous evaluation and feedback are crucial aspects of successful habit stacking. Regular monitoring, feedback loops, and evaluation processes allow organizations to assess the effectiveness of the habit stack, identify areas for improvement, and make necessary adjustments. This lesson emphasizes the need for a feedback-driven approach that encourages ongoing learning and refinement of the habit stacking implementation.

Lesson 5: Cultivating a Supportive Organizational Culture

The case studies highlight the importance of fostering a supportive organizational culture to drive successful habit stacking. Organizations that create an environment that values and reinforces the new behaviors significantly enhance the chances of sustained change. By celebrating successes, recognizing achievements, and promoting collaboration, organizations can cultivate a culture that supports and encourages habit stacking efforts.

Key Takeaway 1: Start Small and Scale Up

A key takeaway from the case studies is the value of starting small and gradually scaling up habit stacking efforts. Beginning with small, achievable habit stacks allows for early wins, builds momentum, and increases confidence. As the habit stacking process gains traction, organizations can expand and incorporate more complex habit stacks, addressing larger goals and broader organizational objectives.

Key Takeaway 2: Collaboration and Communication are Key

Effective collaboration and communication are critical components of successful habit stacking. The case studies demonstrate the importance of involving all relevant stakeholders in the habit stacking process, encouraging open dialogue, and fostering a collaborative approach. Clear and transparent communication ensures that everyone is aligned, engaged, and motivated to drive the desired change.

Key Takeaway 3: Embrace Flexibility & Adaptability

Flexibility and adaptability are key takeaways from the case studies. Organizations need to be open to adjusting their habit stacks based on feedback and evolving circumstances. Embracing flexibility allows for continuous improvement and ensures that habit stacking remains relevant and effective in dynamic environments.

Key Takeaway 4: Persistence and Patience

Implementing habit stacking requires persistence and patience. Sustainable change takes time, and organizations must remain committed to the process despite challenges or setbacks. The case studies highlight the importance of perseverance, resilience, and a long-term perspective in achieving successful habit stacking outcomes.

The case studies presented throughout this book offer valuable lessons and key takeaways for organizations considering the implementation of habit stacking. By clearly identifying target behaviors, leveraging existing routines, providing training and support, and cultivating a supportive organizational culture, organizations can drive meaningful change through habit stacking. Continuous evaluation, collaboration, flexibility, persistence, and patience are essential elements in achieving sustained success with habit stacking. By applying the lessons learned and embracing the key takeaways, organizations can harness the power of habit stacking to drive positive transformation and achieve their desired outcomes.

CHAPTER 16

TOOLS AND FRAMEWORKS FOR EFFECTIVE CHANGE MANAGEMENT

Change management is a complex process that requires careful planning, execution, and monitoring to ensure successful outcomes. In this chapter, we will explore various tools and frameworks that can assist organizations in effectively managing change initiatives. These tools and frameworks provide guidance, structure, and support to navigate the complexities of change management and drive successful outcomes.

Kotter's 8-Step Change Model

Kotter's 8-Step Change Model, developed by renowned change management expert John Kotter, provides a comprehensive framework for managing change. The model includes steps such as creating a sense of urgency, forming a guiding coalition, developing a vision and strategy, empowering employees, and sustaining the change. This framework emphasizes the importance of engaging stakeholders, building a shared vision, and establishing a supportive culture to drive successful change initiatives.

ADKAR Model

The ADKAR Model, developed by Prosci, is a goal-oriented approach that focuses on individual change management. It highlights five key elements: Awareness, Desire, Knowledge, Ability, and Reinforcement. This model recognizes that successful change occurs when individuals have the awareness and desire to change, possess the necessary knowledge and skills, and receive reinforcement and support throughout the process. The ADKAR Model provides a practical framework for addressing individual resistance and facilitating successful change adoption.

Lewin's Change Management Model

Lewin's Change Management Model, developed by psychologist Kurt Lewin, is based on the concept of unfreezing, changing, and refreezing. This model suggests that change involves unfreezing existing behaviors and mindsets, introducing, and implementing the desired change, and refreezing the new behaviors and practices as the new norm. Lewin's model emphasizes the need for effective communication, collaboration, and reinforcement to ensure lasting change.

McKinsey 7-S Framework

The McKinsey 7-S Framework is a holistic approach that focuses on seven key elements: Strategy, Structure, Systems, Shared Values, Skills, Style, and Staff. This framework highlights the interconnectedness of these elements and emphasizes the need for alignment to drive successful change. By assessing and aligning these seven elements, organizations can ensure that their change initiatives are supported by the right strategies, structures, systems, and cultural values.

SWOT Analysis

A SWOT (Strengths, Weaknesses, Opportunities, and Threats) analysis is a widely used tool for assessing the internal and external factors that can impact change initiatives. By identifying and evaluating strengths, weaknesses, opportunities, and threats, organizations gain valuable insights into the current situation and potential challenges and opportunities related to the change. SWOT analysis provides a structured approach to understanding the organizational context and developing strategies to mitigate risks and leverage strengths.

Communication and Engagement Tools

Effective communication and stakeholder engagement are crucial for successful change management. Various tools can facilitate these aspects, including communication plans, stakeholder analysis matrices, and engagement surveys. These tools help organizations identify key stakeholders, develop tailored communication strategies, establish feedback loops, and ensure that messages are effectively delivered and received throughout the change process.

Project Management Tools

Project management tools, such as Gantt charts, project plans, and task management software, play a vital role in change management. These tools help organizations establish clear timelines, allocate resources, track progress, and ensure accountability. Effective project management ensures that change initiatives are well-structured, deadlines are met, and milestones are achieved, fostering successful change implementation.

Performance Measurement and Evaluation Tools

Performance measurement and evaluation tools, such as Key Performance Indicators (KPIs), balanced scorecards, and feedback mechanisms, enable organizations to track and evaluate the impact of change initiatives. These tools provide valuable data and insights on the effectiveness of the change, allowing organizations to make informed decisions, refine strategies, and sustain successful change outcomes.

Conclusion

Effective change management requires the use of appropriate tools and frameworks to navigate the complexities of organizational change. The tools and frameworks discussed in this chapter, including Kotter's 8-Step Change Model, the ADKAR Model, Lewin's Change Management Model, the McKinsey 7-S Framework, SWOT analysis, communication and engagement tools, project management tools, and performance measurement and evaluation tools, offer valuable guidance and support throughout the change management process. By leveraging these tools, organizations can enhance their change management efforts, increase the chances of successful outcomes, and drive sustainable change within their organizations.

CHAPTER 17

THE CHANGE MANAGEMENT FRAMEWORK: A STEP-BY-STEP GUIDE

Change is an inevitable aspect of organizational growth and evolution. However, managing change effectively requires a structured approach that addresses the complexities and challenges that arise during the process. In this chapter, we will provide a step-by-step guide to the change management framework, offering organizations a comprehensive roadmap to navigate change successfully.

Step 1: Establish the Need for Change

The first step in the change management framework is to establish the need for change. This involves conducting a thorough assessment of the current state, identifying areas that require improvement or adaptation, and defining the objectives of the change initiative. Clear and compelling reasons for change must be communicated to stakeholders to generate buy-in and support.

Step 2: Create a Change Management Team

Forming a change management team is essential to drive and support the change initiative. This team should consist of key stakeholders who possess the necessary expertise, influence, and knowledge of the organization. The team will be responsible for developing the change strategy, managing communication, and addressing resistance throughout the process.

Step 3: Develop a Change Management Plan

A robust change management plan outlines the approach, timeline, and resources required for successful change implementation. This plan should address communication strategies, training and development needs, and risk mitigation strategies. The plan should also consider the impact of the change on individuals, teams, and the organization.

Step 4: Communicate Effectively

Communication plays a vital role in change management. Clear, consistent, and timely communication helps stakeholders understand the rationale behind the change, its impact, and their role in the process. The change management team should develop a comprehensive communication plan that includes regular updates, feedback mechanisms, and opportunities for open dialogue.

Step 5: Empower and Engage Employees

Empowering and engaging employees is crucial to ensure their commitment and active participation in the change process. This involves providing opportunities for input and involvement, encouraging innovation and creativity, and recognizing and rewarding contributions. By involving employees in decision-making and fostering a culture of ownership, organizations can harness the collective intelligence and potential for successful change.

Step 6: Provide Training and Support

Change often requires individuals and teams to acquire new skills and knowledge. Providing comprehensive training and support is critical for facilitating the transition. The change management team should assess the training needs, develop tailored programs, and ensure that employees have the resources and support required to adapt to the change successfully.

Step 7: Address Resistance

Resistance to change is a common challenge that organizations face. It is important to address resistance proactively and empathetically. The change management team should identify potential sources of resistance, communicate the benefits of the change, and address concerns and objections through active listening, clarification, and transparent dialogue. Building trust and fostering a safe environment for expressing concerns can help alleviate resistance and increase acceptance of the change.

Step 8: Monitor and Evaluate Progress

Monitoring and evaluating the progress of the change initiative is essential to assess its effectiveness and make necessary adjustments. Key performance indicators (KPIs) should be established to measure the impact of the change on various aspects of the organization. Regular feedback, surveys, and performance reviews can provide valuable insights into the success of the change effort and help identify areas for improvement.

Step 9: Sustain the Change

Sustaining the change requires embedding new behaviors, processes, and systems into the organizational culture. This involves reinforcing the change through recognition, rewards, and ongoing support. The change management team should ensure that the change becomes the new norm and is integrated into day-to-day operations. Regular communication and feedback loops help reinforce the change and address any emerging challenges.

Step 10: Learn and Adapt

Change is a continuous process, and organizations must embrace a culture of learning and adaptation. Reflecting on the change management effort, identifying lessons learned, and capturing best practices are essential for future change initiatives. The change management team should document the successes and challenges encountered and use this knowledge to refine and improve their change management approach.

Conclusion

The change management framework provides organizations with a step-by-step guide to navigate the complexities of change. By establishing the need for change, forming a change management team, developing a comprehensive plan, communicating effectively, empowering and engaging employees, providing training and support, addressing resistance, monitoring progress, sustaining the change, and fostering a culture of learning, organizations can increase their chances of successful change implementation. The change management framework serves as a roadmap to guide organizations through the change process, enabling them to adapt, innovate, and thrive in today's dynamic business environment.

CHAPTER 18

IDENTIFYING CRITICAL BEHAVIORS FOR CHANGE AND HABIT STACKING

Implementing effective change within organizations requires a clear understanding of the critical behaviors that need to be addressed and modified. Identifying these behaviors and utilizing habit stacking techniques can significantly enhance the success of change initiatives. This chapter explores the process of identifying critical behaviors for change and demonstrates how habit stacking can be used to foster sustainable change within organizations.

Step 1: Define the Desired Outcomes

To identify critical behaviors for change, organizations must first define the desired outcomes they wish to achieve. This involves aligning the change initiative with strategic goals and considering the specific challenges or areas that need improvement. By clarifying the desired outcomes, organizations can focus on identifying behaviors that directly contribute to those goals.

Step 2: Conduct a Behavior Analysis

A behavior analysis involves observing and analyzing the current behaviors exhibited within the organization. This analysis helps identify the behaviors that may hinder or support the desired outcomes. It is crucial to involve stakeholders at various levels to gain diverse perspectives and a comprehensive understanding of the behaviors that need to be targeted for change.

Step 3: Prioritize Critical Behaviors

Not all behaviors will have equal importance or impact on the desired outcomes. Prioritization is necessary to focus resources and efforts effectively. Organizations should identify the critical behaviors that are most influential in achieving the desired outcomes. These critical behaviors are the ones that, if changed, will have the greatest positive impact on the organization's success.

Step 4: Determine the Barriers and Enablers

Understanding the barriers and enablers associated with the critical behaviors is essential for effective change management. Barriers may include resistance to change, lack of skills or resources, or conflicting incentives. Enablers, on the other hand, are factors that support and encourage the desired behaviors, such as a positive work environment or effective leadership. By identifying these factors, organizations can develop strategies to overcome barriers and enhance enablers during the change process.

Step 5: Apply Habit Stacking

Once the critical behaviors have been identified, habit stacking can be employed as a technique to facilitate behavior change. Habit stacking involves linking new behaviors to existing routines or habits, making the adoption of the desired behaviors more seamless and sustainable. By leveraging existing habits, individuals are more likely to adopt and maintain the new behaviors, as they are integrated into their daily routines.

Step 6: Anchor the Desired Behaviors

To anchor the desired behaviors, organizations must identify existing routines or habits that are closely associated with the critical behaviors. These anchor habits serve as triggers for the desired behaviors, making it easier for individuals to adopt them. For example, if the desired behavior is to improve communication within teams, a routine such as team meetings or project updates can serve as the anchor habit.

Step 7: Provide Training and Support

Successful habit stacking requires providing the necessary training and support to individuals involved in the change process. This includes equipping them with the knowledge and skills required to perform the desired behaviors effectively. Training can take the form of workshops, coaching sessions, or online resources. Ongoing support, such as feedback, reinforcement, and mentoring, helps individuals sustain the new behaviors and overcome any challenges they may encounter.

Step 8: Monitor and Evaluate Progress

Regular monitoring and evaluation are critical to track the progress of the desired behaviors and assess the effectiveness of the habit stacking approach. Key performance indicators (KPIs) can be established to measure the adoption and impact of the critical behaviors. Feedback mechanisms, surveys, and performance reviews provide valuable insights for refinement and improvement.

Step 9: Adapt and Refine the Approach

As the change initiative progresses, it is essential to adapt and refine the approach based on feedback and emerging insights. Organizations should be open to adjusting the habit stack, addressing any barriers or challenges that arise, and incorporating lessons learned along the way. A flexible and adaptive approach allows for continuous improvement and ensures that the critical behaviors remain aligned with the desired outcomes.

Step 10: Sustain the Changed Behaviors

Sustaining the changed behaviors is crucial for long-term success. Organizations should create an environment that supports and reinforces the desired behaviors. This can be achieved through recognition, rewards, and integrating the behaviors into performance management systems and organizational culture. By embedding the changed behaviors into the fabric of the organization, they become the new norm and contribute to a sustained culture of success.

Conclusion

Identifying critical behaviors for change and utilizing habit stacking techniques are vital components of successful change management. By defining desired outcomes, conducting behavior analysis, prioritizing critical behaviors, and addressing barriers and enablers, organizations can lay the foundation for effective behavior change. Applying habit stacking through anchoring desired behaviors to existing routines, providing training and support, monitoring progress, and adapting the approach ensures sustainable change. By identifying the critical behaviors and leveraging habit stacking, organizations can drive successful change initiatives and create a positive and productive work environment.

CHAPTER 19

MAPPING EXISTING HABITS AND ROUTINES WITHIN THE ORGANIZATION

Understanding the existing habits and routines within an organization is a crucial step in the change management process. Mapping these habits and routines provides valuable insights into the behaviors that shape the organization's culture and operations. This chapter explores the importance of mapping existing habits and routines, the benefits it offers, and provides a step-by-step guide to effectively map habits and routines within the organization.

Why Map Existing Habits and Routines?

Mapping existing habits and routines serves several important purposes in the change management process:

Awareness: Mapping habits and routines brings awareness to the current behaviors within the organization. It helps leaders and change agents identify patterns, both positive and negative, that influence the organization's performance, productivity, and culture.

Alignment: Understanding existing habits and routines allows organizations to align change initiatives with the existing ways of working. This alignment helps in designing change strategies that are more likely to be accepted and integrated into the organization's daily operations.

Identification of Anchor Habits: Mapping habits and routines helps identify anchor habits that can be leveraged for habit stacking. Anchor habits are existing routines that can serve as triggers for new desired behaviors, making change adoption more seamless and sustainable.

Change Planning: Mapping habits and routines provides a solid foundation for effective change planning. It allows organizations to identify the behaviors that need to be modified, the areas where change is most needed, and the potential challenges that may arise during the change process.

Step-by-Step Guide to Mapping Existing Habits and Routines

Step 1: Identify the Scope

Define the scope of the mapping exercise. Determine whether you will focus on the entire organization, specific departments, or targeted processes. Clarify the objectives and outcomes you want to achieve through the mapping process.

Step 2: Gather Data

Collect data through observations, interviews, surveys, and document analysis. Engage with employees at various levels to gain a comprehensive understanding of their daily routines and habits. Consider using tools such as questionnaires or focus groups to gather insights into the behaviors and routines prevalent within the organization.

Step 3: Analyze the Data

Analyze the data collected to identify recurring patterns and common routines. Look for habits that have a significant impact on productivity, collaboration, and overall performance. Identify routines that contribute to positive outcomes as well as those that may hinder progress or innovation.

Step 4: Categorize and Prioritize

Categorize the identified habits and routines based on their impact and alignment with the desired change. Prioritize the habits and routines that are most relevant to the change initiative and have the potential to influence the desired outcomes. This prioritization helps in focusing efforts and resources effectively.

Step 5: Map the Habits and Routines

Create a visual representation of the mapped habits and routines. This can be done through flowcharts, diagrams, or process maps. Clearly indicate the sequence of activities, dependencies, and relationships among the identified habits and routines. Visual mapping helps in understanding the overall flow and interconnectedness of behaviors within the organization.

Step 6: Identify Anchor Habits

Based on the mapped habits and routines, identify anchor habits that can serve as triggers for new desired behaviors. These anchor habits should be activities that occur regularly and have the potential to influence other behaviors. Anchor habits provide an opportunity for habit stacking, linking new behaviors to existing routines for seamless adoption.

Step 7: Evaluate the Impact

Evaluate the impact of the identified habits and routines on the organization's goals and desired outcomes. Assess whether they are aligned with the organization's values, vision, and strategic objectives. Identify any gaps or misalignments that need to be addressed as part of the change initiative.

Step 8: Engage Stakeholders

Engage key stakeholders, including employees, managers, and leaders, in the mapping process. Seek their input and insights to validate and refine the mapped habits and routines. Encourage open dialogue and collaboration to ensure a comprehensive understanding of the existing behaviors.

Step 9: Communicate and Share Findings

Communicate the findings of the mapping exercise to all relevant stakeholders. Share the visual representation of the mapped habits and routines, highlighting the identified anchor habits and their potential influence on the desired change. Ensure that the communication is clear, transparent, and promotes understanding and buy-in for the change initiative.

Step 10: Update and Iterate

Habits and routines within organizations are dynamic and may evolve over time. Continuously update and iterate the mapped habits and routines as the organization progresses through the change process. Regularly revisit the mapping exercise to assess the effectiveness of the change efforts and identify any emerging behaviors that need to be addressed.

Benefits of Mapping Existing Habits and Routines

Mapping existing habits and routines within the organization offers several benefits:

Insights for Change: Mapping provides valuable insights into the behaviors that influence organizational culture and performance. It guides change efforts by identifying the specific habits and routines that need to be targeted for modification.

Alignment and Integration: By mapping existing habits and routines, change initiatives can be aligned with the organization's daily operations and integrated into existing workflows. This alignment increases the likelihood of successful adoption and sustainability of the desired behaviors.

Habit Stacking Opportunities: Mapping helps identify anchor habits that can be leveraged for habit stacking. By linking new behaviors to existing routines, habit stacking enhances the adoption and reinforcement of desired behaviors.

Targeted Interventions: Mapping allows organizations to prioritize their interventions by focusing on the most influential and critical habits and routines. This targeted approach maximizes the impact of change efforts and optimizes resource allocation.

Continuous Improvement: Mapping habits and routines is an iterative process that enables organizations to continuously assess and refine their understanding of behaviors. It supports ongoing improvement and enables organizations to adapt to evolving needs and challenges.

Conclusion

Mapping existing habits and routines within the organization is a fundamental step in the change management process. It provides valuable insights into the behaviors that shape the organization's culture and operations. By effectively mapping habits and routines, organizations can identify critical behaviors for change, leverage anchor habits for habit stacking, and align change initiatives with existing ways of working. This mapping process enhances the effectiveness and sustainability of change efforts and promotes a culture of continuous improvement within the organization.

CHAPTER 20

STRATEGIES FOR INTEGRATING NEW BEHAVIORS THROUGH HABIT STACKING

Habit stacking is a powerful technique that leverages existing habits and routines to integrate new behaviors seamlessly into individuals' daily lives. This chapter explores strategies for effectively integrating new behaviors through habit stacking. By understanding and applying these strategies, organizations can enhance the adoption and sustainability of desired behaviors, driving successful change initiatives.

Start Small and Build Momentum: When integrating new behaviors through habit stacking, it is essential to start small and build momentum gradually. Begin by introducing one or two new behaviors that are easily achievable and aligned with the desired change. By focusing on small wins, individuals are more likely to adopt the new behaviors and build confidence in their ability to change. As these new behaviors become habitual, individuals can gradually incorporate additional behaviors over time.

Identify and Leverage Existing Cues: Existing cues or triggers are essential for successful habit stacking. Identify the cues associated with the anchor habit and link them to the desired new behavior. For example, if the anchor habit is brewing a cup of coffee in the morning, the cue could be the sound of the coffee machine. Linking a new behavior, such as spending five minutes reviewing a to-do list, to the coffee brewing routine creates an association that prompts the desired behavior.

Align Behaviors with Natural Sequences: Integrating new behaviors into natural sequences or routines can enhance habit stacking. Identify existing sequences of behaviors that occur in a specific order and align the new behavior within that sequence. For instance, if employees routinely check their emails in the morning, aligning the new behavior of setting daily priorities immediately after checking emails ensures it becomes part of their natural workflow.

Provide Clear Instructions and Reminders: Clear instructions and reminders are vital for reinforcing new behaviors. Clearly communicate the specific steps involved in performing the desired behavior and provide reminders through various means, such as visual cues, written instructions, or digital prompts. This ensures that individuals have a clear understanding of what needs to be done and helps them stay on track with their new habit.

Use Positive Reinforcement and Rewards: Positive reinforcement and rewards are powerful motivators for behavior change. Celebrate individuals' progress and achievements when they successfully adopt and maintain the new behavior. Rewards can be as simple as verbal praise, recognition in team meetings, or small incentives. By associating positive experiences with the new behavior, individuals are more likely to continue practicing it and reinforce the habit.

Build Accountability and Support Systems: Creating accountability and support systems is crucial for sustaining new behaviors. Encourage individuals to share their progress, challenges, and experiences with their peers or through dedicated forums. This fosters a sense of accountability and allows individuals to support and motivate each other in adopting and maintaining the new behavior. Regular check-ins, coaching, or mentorship can also provide additional support and guidance.

Provide Training and Skill Development: Integrating new behaviors often requires individuals to acquire new skills and knowledge. Provide comprehensive training and skill development opportunities to equip individuals with the necessary capabilities to perform the desired behavior effectively. Training programs can range from workshops, e-learning modules, to on-the-job coaching. Continuous learning and skill development ensure individuals are confident and competent in practicing the new behavior.

Adapt and Iterate as Needed: Flexibility and adaptability are key to successful habit stacking. Monitor the integration of new behaviors and be open to adjusting as needed. Pay attention to feedback, challenges, and emerging insights from individuals practicing the new behavior. This allows for continuous improvement and refinement of the habit stack, ensuring that it remains relevant and effective in driving change.

Create a Supportive Environment: A supportive environment is critical for integrating new behaviors. Foster a culture that encourages and reinforces the desired behaviors. Ensure that organizational structures, systems, and processes support the habit stacking approach. Provide resources, tools, and technologies that facilitate the adoption and practice of the new behaviors. When individuals feel supported and empowered, they are more likely to embrace and sustain the change.

Communicate and Share Success Stories: Communication plays a vital role in habit stacking and behavior integration. Regularly communicate the progress and successes of individuals who have successfully integrated the new behaviors through habit stacking. Share success stories, best practices, and lessons learned to inspire and motivate others. This creates a positive narrative around the desired behaviors and encourages wider adoption within the organization.

Conclusion

Integrating new behaviors through habit stacking is a powerful strategy for driving successful change initiatives. By applying effective strategies, such as starting small, leveraging existing cues, aligning with natural sequences, providing clear instructions and reminders, using positive reinforcement, building accountability and support systems, providing training, adapting as needed, creating a supportive environment, and communicating success stories, organizations can increase the adoption and sustainability of desired behaviors. Habit stacking allows for seamless integration of new behaviors into individuals' routines, leading to lasting change and improved organizational performance. By employing these strategies, organizations can harness the power of habit stacking to drive transformative change and cultivate a culture of continuous improvement.

CHAPTER 21

COMMUNICATING AND REINFORCING CHANGE THROUGH HABIT STACKING

Effective communication and reinforcement are essential for driving successful change initiatives within organizations. When combined with habit stacking, communication becomes a powerful tool for integrating new behaviors seamlessly into individuals' routines. This chapter explores strategies for communicating and reinforcing change through habit stacking, emphasizing the importance of clear messaging, ongoing support, and consistent reinforcement to drive sustainable change.

Develop a Clear Communication Plan

A clear communication plan is vital for effectively conveying the change message to all stakeholders. Outline the key objectives, messages, and target audiences for the communication effort. Consider using multiple communication channels, such as team meetings, email updates, newsletters, and digital platforms, to ensure widespread dissemination of information. The communication plan should also include a feedback mechanism to encourage open dialogue and address any concerns or questions.

Align Communication with Anchor Habits

When communicating change, it is crucial to align the messaging with the anchor habits used in the habit stacking approach. Highlight the connection between the existing routines and the desired change behaviors. By emphasizing how the new behaviors complement and enhance the existing habits, individuals are more likely to understand and embrace the change.

Make Messages Relevant and Meaningful

To effectively communicate change, make the messages relevant and meaningful to the individuals involved. Tailor the messages to address their specific roles, responsibilities, and concerns. Explain the rationale behind the change and how it aligns with the organization's goals and vision. Emphasize the benefits and positive outcomes that the change will bring, inspiring individuals to adopt the new behaviors.

Utilize Multiple Communication Channels

Utilize a variety of communication channels to reach individuals at different levels and in different departments or teams. This ensures that the change messages are delivered effectively and consistently throughout the organization. Consider using face-to-face meetings, presentations, videos, intranet portals, and social media platforms to reinforce the change messages and keep individuals informed.

Encourage Two-Way Communication

Effective communication is a two-way process. Encourage individuals to provide feedback, ask questions, and share their thoughts and concerns. This can be done through surveys, focus groups, suggestion boxes, or dedicated communication channels. Actively listen to their feedback, address any issues promptly, and provide transparent and honest responses. Two-way communication builds trust, engagement, and a sense of ownership in the change process.

Provide Ongoing Support and Resources

Support and resources are essential for individuals to adopt and sustain the new behaviors. Provide training programs, job aids, and reference materials that help individuals understand and practice the desired behaviors effectively. Offer coaching, mentoring, or peer support to address any challenges or questions that may arise during the change process. Ongoing support ensures that individuals feel equipped and empowered to embrace the change.

Reinforce Desired Behaviors with Recognition and Rewards

Recognition and rewards play a crucial role in reinforcing desired behaviors and sustaining change. Implement a system that acknowledges and celebrates individuals who consistently practice the new behaviors through habit stacking. This can include formal recognition programs, verbal praise, certificates, or incentives that align with the organization's culture and values. Recognition and rewards create a positive reinforcement loop that motivates individuals to continue the desired behaviors.

Lead by Example

Leaders and managers have a significant influence on the adoption of new behaviors. They should lead by example and demonstrate the desired behaviors themselves. This sets a powerful precedent and reinforces the importance of the change throughout the organization. Leaders should actively participate in habit stacking and communicate their own experiences and successes, inspiring others to follow suit.

Foster a Learning Culture

Change is an ongoing process, and individuals need to continuously learn and adapt. Foster a learning culture that encourages individuals to seek knowledge, share best practices, and engage in continuous improvement. Provide opportunities for individuals to learn from each other, share their experiences, and participate in communities of practice. Learning opportunities help individuals refine their habits and routines, driving sustainable change.

Continuously Monitor and Adapt

Monitor the progress and effectiveness of the change effort and adapt the communication and reinforcement strategies as needed. Regularly collect feedback, assess the adoption of the new behaviors, and identify any barriers or challenges that may hinder change. Use this information to refine the communication approach, reinforce positive behaviors, and address any gaps or concerns.

Conclusion

Effective communication and reinforcement are critical for driving successful change initiatives within organizations. When combined with habit stacking, communication becomes a powerful tool for integrating new behaviors seamlessly into individuals' routines. By developing a clear communication plan, aligning messages with anchor habits, making messages relevant and meaningful, utilizing multiple communication channels, encouraging two-way communication, providing ongoing support, reinforcing behaviors with recognition and rewards, leading by example, fostering a learning culture, and continuously monitoring and adapting, organizations can drive sustainable change and create a culture of continuous improvement. Through effective communication and reinforcement, habit stacking becomes a powerful mechanism for embedding new behaviors, leading to improved organizational performance, and lasting change.

CHAPTER 22

IMPLEMENTING HABIT STACKING IN ORGANIZATIONS

Habit stacking is a powerful technique that can drive behavior change and facilitate the adoption of new habits within organizations. By leveraging existing routines and habits, habit stacking makes it easier for individuals to integrate new behaviors seamlessly into their daily lives. This chapter explores the process of implementing habit stacking in organizations, highlighting key considerations and strategies for successful adoption.

Assess Readiness for Change

Before implementing habit stacking, it is important to assess the organization's readiness for change. Evaluate the organizational culture, leadership support, and employees' willingness to embrace new behaviors. Identify any potential barriers or challenges that may hinder the successful adoption of habit stacking. This assessment provides valuable insights for developing a tailored approach to implementing habit stacking.

Define the Desired Behaviors

Clearly define the desired behaviors that the organization aims to promote through habit stacking. These behaviors should align with the organization's goals and values. It is important to be specific and measurable in defining the behaviors, as this helps in tracking progress and evaluating the effectiveness of habit stacking. Examples of desired behaviors could include improved communication, enhanced collaboration, or increased productivity.

Identify Anchor Habits

Identify the existing routines and habits within the organization that can serve as anchor habits for habit stacking. These anchor habits should be regularly practiced by individuals and have a strong connection to the desired behaviors. For example, if the desired behavior is to encourage knowledge sharing, an anchor habit could be the routine of team meetings or project debriefs. Identify anchor habits that are prevalent and widely adopted across teams or departments.

Link New Behaviors to Anchor Habits

Once the anchor habits have been identified, establish the link between the new desired behaviors and the anchor habits. Clearly communicate how the new behaviors can be integrated into the existing routines and how they complement and enhance the anchor habits. This linkage ensures that individuals understand how the new behaviors fit into their daily routines and increases the likelihood of successful adoption through habit stacking.

Provide Training and Education

Implementing habit stacking may require individuals to acquire new skills and knowledge. Provide comprehensive training and education programs to equip individuals with the necessary capabilities to perform the new behaviors effectively. Training should focus on the specific behaviors being targeted and provide practical guidance on how to integrate them into existing routines. By providing the necessary training, individuals feel confident and empowered to practice the new behaviors through habit stacking.

Establish Accountability and Support Systems

Accountability and support systems are essential for sustaining habit stacking within organizations. Establish mechanisms for tracking progress and providing ongoing support. This can include regular check-ins, performance reviews, or feedback loops. Hold individuals accountable for practicing the desired behaviors and provide constructive feedback to support their efforts. Peer support and mentorship programs can also play a crucial role in fostering a culture of accountability and providing additional support for habit stacking.

Create a Positive Reinforcement Culture

Positive reinforcement is a powerful tool for sustaining behavior change. Create a culture of positive reinforcement by recognizing and rewarding individuals who successfully practice the desired behaviors through habit stacking. Celebrate their achievements and share success stories to inspire others. This creates a positive feedback loop that encourages individuals to continue adopting the new behaviors.

Foster Continuous Improvement

Habit stacking should not be seen as a one-time initiative but as an ongoing process of continuous improvement. Encourage individuals and teams to reflect on their habit stacking practices, share lessons learned, and identify areas for refinement. Foster a culture of learning and experimentation, allowing individuals to try new approaches and adapt their habit stacking techniques based on feedback and evolving needs.

Monitor and Evaluate Progress

Regularly monitor and evaluate the progress of habit stacking within the organization. Establish key performance indicators (KPIs) to measure the adoption and impact of the desired behaviors. Collect feedback from individuals and teams to assess the effectiveness of habit stacking and identify any barriers or challenges that need to be addressed. Use this information to make data-driven decisions and refine the implementation of habit stacking.

Communicate and Share Best Practices

Communication plays a crucial role in implementing habit stacking effectively. Regularly communicate the benefits of habit stacking, share success stories, and highlight best practices. Use various communication channels, such as team meetings, newsletters, or digital platforms, to reach a wide audience. Encourage individuals and teams to share their experiences, challenges, and lessons learned, fostering a collaborative environment where knowledge and insights can be shared.

Implementing habit stacking in organizations offers a powerful approach to drive behavior change and foster the adoption of new habits. By assessing readiness, defining desired behaviors, identifying anchor habits, linking new behaviors, providing training and education, establishing accountability and support systems, creating a positive reinforcement culture, fostering continuous improvement, monitoring progress, and communicating effectively, organizations can successfully implement habit stacking and create a culture of sustained behavior change. Through habit stacking, organizations can transform their routines and habits, driving positive outcomes and enhancing individual and organizational performance.

CHAPTER 23

ASSESSING ORGANIZATIONAL READINESS FOR HABIT STACKING

Before implementing habit stacking as a strategy for behavior change within an organization, it is crucial to assess the organizational readiness. Assessing readiness helps identify potential barriers, determine the level of support, and plan for successful adoption of habit stacking. This chapter explores the importance of assessing organizational readiness and provides a step-by-step guide to evaluate the organization's readiness for habit stacking.

Why Assess Organizational Readiness for Habit Stacking?

Assessing organizational readiness for habit stacking offers several benefits:

Identifying Barriers: Assessing readiness helps identify potential barriers or challenges that may hinder the successful implementation of habit stacking. It allows organizations to proactively address these barriers and develop strategies to overcome them.

Establishing Support: Evaluating readiness helps determine the level of support from key stakeholders, including leaders, managers, and employees. Identifying supportive individuals and securing their buy-in increases the likelihood of successful adoption of habit stacking.

Planning and Resource Allocation: Assessing readiness provides insights into the organization's capacity and resources. It helps in planning and allocating resources effectively to support the implementation of habit stacking.

Tailoring Approach: Evaluating readiness helps organizations tailor their approach to habit stacking based on the organization's unique context, culture, and challenges. This ensures that the implementation plan aligns with the organization's specific needs and maximizes the chances of success.

Step-by-Step Guide to Assess Organizational Readiness for Habit Stacking

Step 1: Define Objectives and Desired Outcomes

Clearly define the objectives and desired outcomes of habit stacking within the organization. This involves determining the specific behaviors or habits that need to be targeted for change. Align these objectives with the organization's overall goals and strategic priorities.

Step 2: Identify Key Stakeholders

Identify the key stakeholders who will be involved in or impacted by habit stacking. This includes leaders, managers, teams, and individuals across different levels and departments. Engage these stakeholders in the assessment process to gather diverse perspectives and ensure their active participation in the change effort.

Step 3: Assess Organizational Culture

Evaluate the organizational culture to determine its readiness for habit stacking. Assess factors such as openness to change, willingness to experiment, and the organization's history with previous change initiatives. Identify cultural characteristics that may support or hinder habit stacking and consider how to leverage or address these factors during implementation.

Step 4: Evaluate Leadership Support

Assess the level of support and commitment from leaders within the organization. Leaders play a crucial role in driving change and setting the tone for habit stacking. Evaluate their understanding of habit stacking, their willingness to champion the initiative, and their ability to provide the necessary resources and support.

Step 5: Analyze Employee Engagement

Evaluate the level of employee engagement and readiness for change. Assess factors such as employee motivation, receptiveness to new ideas, and willingness to participate in behavior change initiatives. Consider conducting surveys, focus groups, or interviews to gather insights into employee attitudes and perceptions related to habit stacking.

Step 6: Assess Resources and Capacity

Evaluate the availability of resources and capacity to support habit stacking. This includes assessing the availability of time, personnel, technology, and training resources required for successful implementation. Identify any resource gaps or constraints and develop strategies to address them.

Step 7: Identify Potential Barriers

Identify potential barriers or challenges that may impede the successful adoption of habit stacking. These barriers can include resistance to change, lack of awareness or understanding, competing priorities, or inadequate communication channels. Identify specific strategies to address each barrier and mitigate its impact on habit stacking.

Step 8: Evaluate Communication Channels

Assess the effectiveness of existing communication channels within the organization. Evaluate the frequency, clarity, and accessibility of communication channels to ensure they can effectively support habit stacking. Identify any gaps in communication and develop a plan to enhance communication strategies and tools.

Step 9: Determine Training and Support Needs

Evaluate the organization's training and support needs for habit stacking. Assess the level of knowledge and skills required to implement habit stacking effectively. Identify potential training programs, coaching, or mentoring opportunities to develop the necessary capabilities within the organization.

Step 10: Develop an Implementation Plan

Based on the assessment findings, develop a comprehensive implementation plan for habit stacking. This plan should address the identified barriers, leverage existing support, allocate necessary resources, and outline clear steps for implementation. It should also include a timeline, communication strategy, training programs, and mechanisms for monitoring and evaluation.

Assessing organizational readiness for habit stacking is a critical step in the successful implementation of behavior change initiatives within organizations. By evaluating the organizational culture, leadership support, employee engagement, resources, potential barriers, communication channels, training and support needs, organizations can identify strengths, weaknesses, and areas of improvement for habit stacking. This assessment process ensures that the implementation of habit stacking is tailored to the organization's unique context and increases the chances of successful adoption and sustainable change. By understanding the readiness factors and planning accordingly, organizations can maximize the benefits of habit stacking and drive positive behavior change within their workforce.

CHAPTER 24

OVERCOMING CHALLENGES AND RESISTANCE IN IMPLEMENTING HABIT STACKING

Implementing habit stacking as a strategy for behavior change within organizations can face various challenges and encounter resistance from individuals and teams. Overcoming these challenges is crucial for the successful adoption and sustainability of habit stacking. This chapter explores common challenges and resistance faced during the implementation of habit stacking and provides strategies to overcome them effectively.

Understanding Challenges and Resistance

Lack of Awareness and Understanding: One of the primary challenges in implementing habit stacking is a lack of awareness and understanding among individuals and teams. They may not be familiar with the concept of habit stacking or the benefits it offers. Overcoming this challenge requires effective communication and education to ensure individuals understand the purpose, process, and value of habit stacking.

Resistance to Change: Resistance to change is a common barrier when introducing new behaviors through habit stacking. Individuals may be resistant to altering their established routines or hesitant to adopt new habits. This resistance can stem from fear of the unknown, concerns about increased workload, or a preference for familiar ways of doing things. Overcoming resistance to change requires addressing individuals' concerns, providing reassurance, and creating a supportive environment.

Lack of Leadership Support

Without strong leadership support, implementing habit stacking can be challenging. Leaders play a crucial role in driving and championing the change effort. Their support and commitment inspire others to embrace the new behaviors. Overcoming this challenge involves engaging leaders early in the process, communicating the benefits of habit stacking, and securing their active involvement and endorsement.

Competing Priorities

Organizations often have competing priorities and limited resources. This can lead to challenges in allocating time and resources to habit stacking initiatives. Overcoming this challenge requires aligning habit stacking with strategic priorities, demonstrating its value in achieving organizational goals, and advocating for dedicated resources.

Lack of Accountability

The absence of accountability can undermine the successful implementation of habit stacking. Without clear accountability measures, individuals may struggle to maintain consistency and sustain the new habits. Overcoming this challenge involves establishing mechanisms for tracking and evaluating the adoption of new behaviors. This can include regular check-ins, performance reviews, or peer accountability partnerships.

Strategies to Overcome Challenges and Resistance

Build Awareness and Provide Education: To overcome the lack of awareness and understanding, organizations should provide comprehensive education and communication about habit stacking. Clearly explain the concept, its benefits, and how it aligns with the organization's goals. Share success stories and case studies to illustrate the positive impact of habit stacking on individuals and teams.

Create a Compelling Case for Change: To address resistance to change, organizations should create a compelling case for habit stacking. Highlight the reasons for the change, such as improving efficiency, enhancing teamwork, or driving innovation. Clearly communicate the benefits and opportunities that habit stacking brings, addressing any concerns or fears individuals may have.

Engage and Involve Stakeholders: Engaging and involving stakeholders is crucial in overcoming challenges and resistance. Seek input and feedback from individuals and teams affected by habit stacking. Involve them in the decision-making process, ensuring their perspectives and concerns are heard. By involving stakeholders, organizations can foster a sense of ownership and commitment to the change effort.

Provide Training and Support: To address resistance and build competency, organizations should provide training and support for habit stacking. Offer workshops, seminars, or coaching sessions to help individuals understand the process and develop the necessary skills. Provide ongoing support through resources, job aids, and access to mentors or coaches who can guide individuals in integrating new habits effectively.

Foster a Supportive Environment: Creating a supportive environment is essential in overcoming challenges and resistance. Establish a culture that values experimentation, continuous improvement, and learning. Encourage collaboration and knowledge sharing among individuals and teams practicing habit stacking. Recognize and celebrate successes to reinforce the adoption of new behaviors and create a positive reinforcement loop.

Address Concerns and Provide Reassurance: Addressing concerns and providing reassurance is crucial in overcoming resistance to habit stacking. Take the time to listen to individuals' apprehensions and provide clear explanations and solutions. Demonstrate empathy and understanding, ensuring individuals feel supported and that their concerns are acknowledged. Communicate the potential benefits and address any perceived risks or challenges associated with habit stacking.

Lead by Example: Leaders must lead by example and demonstrate the desired behaviors through habit stacking. Their commitment and consistent practice of the new habits create a culture of change and inspire others to follow suit. Leaders should openly communicate their experiences, challenges, and successes with habit stacking, encouraging others to embrace the change.

Monitor Progress and Provide Feedback: Regularly monitor progress and provide feedback to individuals and teams practicing habit stacking. Celebrate achievements and provide constructive feedback to support ongoing improvement. This feedback loop helps individuals stay on track, make necessary adjustments, and reinforce positive behaviors.

Adapt and Evolve: Flexibility and adaptability are crucial in overcoming challenges and resistance. Recognize that habit stacking may require adjustments based on feedback and changing circumstances. Continuously evaluate the effectiveness of the chosen habits and adapt the approach as needed. Embrace a learning mindset and foster a culture of continuous improvement.

Conclusion

Implementing habit stacking within organizations can encounter challenges and face resistance. However, by understanding and addressing these challenges, organizations can successfully overcome resistance and foster a culture of behavior change. By building awareness, creating a compelling case for change, engaging stakeholders, providing training and support, fostering a supportive environment, addressing concerns, leading by example, monitoring progress, and embracing adaptability, organizations can navigate the challenges and drive the successful implementation of habit stacking. With perseverance and the right strategies, habit stacking can become a powerful tool for sustainable behavior change within organizations, leading to improved performance and organizational success.

CHAPTER 25

CREATING A CULTURE OF CONTINUOUS IMPROVEMENT THROUGH HABIT STACKING

Creating a culture of continuous improvement is essential for organizations seeking to adapt, innovate, and stay ahead in today's dynamic business landscape. Habit stacking can play a pivotal role in fostering this culture by integrating new behaviors seamlessly into individuals' routines. This chapter explores strategies for creating a culture of continuous improvement through habit stacking, emphasizing the importance of experimentation, learning, and iteration.

Embrace a Growth Mindset: Creating a culture of continuous improvement starts with embracing a growth mindset. Encourage individuals and teams to adopt a belief that their abilities and skills can be developed through dedication and effort. Emphasize that failures and setbacks are opportunities for learning and growth. By fostering a growth mindset, individuals are more likely to embrace habit stacking to improve and evolve.

Establish a Safe and Supportive Environment: To foster continuous improvement, create a safe and supportive environment where individuals feel comfortable taking risks and sharing ideas. Encourage open communication, active listening, and constructive feedback. Celebrate individuals who experiment, learn, and adapt through habit stacking. By creating a psychologically safe space, individuals are more likely to engage in continuous improvement efforts.

Encourage Experimentation and Innovation: Continuous improvement thrives on experimentation and innovation. Encourage individuals and teams to experiment with new habits and approaches through habit stacking. Emphasize the importance of learning from both successes and failures. Encourage individuals to share their learnings and insights, promoting a culture of knowledge sharing and collaboration.

Incorporate Regular Reflection and Review: To cultivate a culture of continuous improvement, build in regular opportunities for reflection and review. Encourage individuals and teams to reflect on their habit stacking practices, identify areas for improvement, and celebrate successes. Provide structured reflection exercises or tools that guide individuals in evaluating their progress and identifying areas for growth.

Foster a Learning Culture: Create a learning culture where continuous learning and development are valued. Encourage individuals to seek out learning opportunities, both within and outside the organization. Provide access to resources, training programs, and knowledge-sharing platforms. Support individuals in acquiring new skills and knowledge that can be integrated into their habit stacking practices.

Establish Feedback Loops: Feedback loops are vital for continuous improvement. Establish mechanisms for regular feedback on habit stacking practices. Encourage individuals and teams to provide feedback on each other's habits, offering constructive suggestions for improvement. Implement regular check-ins and performance reviews that include discussions on habit stacking progress and opportunities for growth.

Recognize and Celebrate Progress: Recognition and celebration are powerful motivators for continuous improvement. Acknowledge and celebrate the progress made by individuals and teams through habit stacking. Highlight success stories and share best practices to inspire others. This recognition reinforces the value of continuous improvement efforts and encourages individuals to continue refining their habits.

Provide Opportunities for Collaboration: Collaboration is a key driver of continuous improvement. Create opportunities for individuals and teams to collaborate and learn from each other's habit stacking practices. Encourage cross-functional collaboration and the sharing of ideas, insights, and challenges. Foster a culture where individuals feel comfortable seeking help, sharing their experiences, and working together to improve collectively.

Promote Agile and Iterative Approaches: Embrace agile and iterative approaches to habit stacking. Encourage individuals to start small, experiment, and iterate their habits based on feedback and outcomes. Emphasize the importance of continuous iteration and refinement to achieve sustained improvement. Encourage individuals to adapt their habit stacking practices as the organization's needs and goals evolve.

Lead by Example: Leaders play a crucial role in creating a culture of continuous improvement. Leaders should model the behaviors they want to see by actively engaging in habit stacking and continuously seeking opportunities for improvement. Encourage leaders to share their habit stacking experiences, challenges, and lessons learned. This transparency and vulnerability inspire others to embrace continuous improvement and habit stacking.

Conclusion

Creating a culture of continuous improvement through habit stacking is a powerful approach for organizations to adapt, innovate, and thrive in a rapidly changing world. By embracing a growth mindset, establishing a safe and supportive environment, encouraging experimentation and innovation, incorporating reflection and review, fostering a learning culture, establishing feedback loops, recognizing progress, promoting collaboration, promoting agile approaches, and leading by example, organizations can foster a culture of continuous improvement. Through habit stacking, individuals and teams integrate new behaviors seamlessly into their routines, driving sustained improvement and organizational success. By cultivating this culture, organizations can foster a dynamic, adaptive, and innovative environment that embraces change and drives continuous growth.

CHAPTER 26

MEASURING THE IMPACT OF HABIT STACKING ON ORGANIZATIONAL CHANGE

Evaluating and measuring the impact of habit stacking on organizational change is crucial for assessing the effectiveness and success of behavior change initiatives. By systematically evaluating the impact, organizations can identify areas of improvement, track progress, and make data-driven decisions to optimize habit stacking strategies. This chapter explores strategies for evaluating and measuring the impact of habit stacking on organizational change, emphasizing the importance of defining metrics, collecting data, and analyzing results.

Define Clear Objectives and Metrics: To effectively evaluate the impact of habit stacking, start by defining clear objectives and metrics. Determine the specific outcomes or behaviors that habit stacking aims to influence. Examples of metrics can include productivity levels, collaboration rates, customer satisfaction scores, or employee engagement levels. Ensure that the chosen metrics align with the overall organizational goals and are measurable.

Establish Baseline Data: Before implementing habit stacking, establish baseline data to serve as a point of comparison for measuring impact. Collect relevant data on the chosen metrics before habit stacking initiatives begin. This baseline data provides a reference point for assessing the changes and improvements brought about by habit stacking.

Collect Quantitative and Qualitative Data: Evaluating the impact of habit stacking requires a combination of quantitative and qualitative data. Quantitative data includes measurable metrics and numerical data points. This can be collected through surveys, assessments, or tracking systems. Qualitative data provides deeper insights into individuals' experiences and perceptions. It can be gathered through interviews, focus groups, or open-ended survey questions. Collecting both types of data provides a comprehensive understanding of the impact of habit stacking.

Use Surveys and Assessments: Surveys and assessments are valuable tools for evaluating the impact of habit stacking. Develop surveys or assessments that capture the targeted behaviors or outcomes influenced by habit stacking. Ensure that the questions are designed to gather specific data aligned with the defined metrics. Use Likert scale or multiple-choice questions to facilitate data analysis and comparison.

Conduct Interviews and Focus Groups: In addition to surveys and assessments, conduct interviews and focus groups to gather qualitative data. Engage individuals and teams who have participated in habit stacking initiatives to understand their experiences, challenges, and perceived impact. Explore their perspectives on changes in behaviors, performance, and overall organizational culture. These insights provide a deeper understanding of the impact beyond numerical metrics.

Analyze Data and Identify Trends: Once data is collected, analyze it to identify trends and patterns. Look for changes in behavior, performance, or other relevant metrics compared to the baseline data. Use statistical analysis techniques to identify significant differences and correlations. Visualize the data through charts, graphs, or dashboards to facilitate interpretation and communication of the results.

Compare Results to Organizational Goals: Compare the results of the evaluation to the organization's goals and objectives. Determine whether the impact of habit stacking aligns with the desired outcomes. Assess whether the changes in behaviors or metrics contribute positively to the organization's overall success. Identify areas of improvement or areas that require further attention.

Continuously Monitor and Track Progress: Evaluation is an ongoing process. Continuously monitor and track the progress of habit stacking initiatives over time. Collect data at regular intervals to measure the sustainability and long-term impact of habit stacking. This monitoring allows organizations to adjust, refine strategies, and address any emerging challenges or opportunities.

Seek Feedback from Participants: To gain valuable insights, seek feedback from participants who have experienced habit stacking. Encourage open dialogue and honest feedback about their experiences, challenges, and suggestions for improvement. Incorporate this feedback into the evaluation process and use it to inform future habit stacking initiatives.

Share Results and Learnings: Share the results and learnings from the evaluation process with relevant stakeholders. Communicate the impact of habit stacking and how it aligns with the organization's goals. Highlight success stories, challenges, and lessons learned. This sharing of results fosters transparency, accountability, and a culture of continuous improvement.

Evaluating and measuring the impact of habit stacking on organizational change provides valuable insights into the effectiveness of behavior change initiatives. By defining clear objectives and metrics, collecting quantitative and qualitative data, conducting surveys and assessments, analyzing data, comparing results to organizational goals, continuously monitoring progress, seeking feedback, and sharing results and learnings, organizations can gain a comprehensive understanding of the impact of habit stacking. This evaluation process enables organizations to optimize habit stacking strategies, make informed decisions, and drive continuous improvement. By measuring and evaluating the impact, organizations can effectively harness the power of habit stacking to drive positive and sustainable change within their workforce.

CHAPTER 27

REVIEW KEY PRINCIPLES OF CHANGE MANAGEMENT AND HABIT STACKING

Throughout this book, we have explored the principles and strategies of change management and habit stacking as powerful approaches for driving successful organizational change. In this final chapter, we will recap the key principles and strategies discussed, highlighting their significance, and providing a comprehensive overview of how they can be applied to create meaningful and lasting change within organizations.

Change Management Principles

Clear Vision and Goals: A clear vision and well-defined goals are the foundation of successful change management. They provide a sense of purpose and direction, guiding individuals and teams towards the desired change outcomes.

Strong Leadership: Effective leadership is critical for driving change. Leaders play a pivotal role in inspiring and motivating individuals, providing guidance, and creating a supportive environment for change.

Stakeholder Engagement: Engaging stakeholders throughout the change process fosters buy-in, ownership, and collaboration. It ensures that diverse perspectives are considered, and potential resistance is addressed.

Communication and Transparency: Clear and consistent communication is essential for creating awareness, understanding, and alignment. Transparent communication builds trust and encourages open dialogue throughout the change journey.

Change Readiness and Adaptability: Organizations must be prepared for change and embrace adaptability. Building change readiness involves assessing the organization's capacity, addressing resistance, and fostering a culture that embraces continuous learning and improvement.

Habit Stacking Principles

Leveraging Existing Routines: Habit stacking capitalizes on existing routines and habits to integrate new behaviors seamlessly. By anchoring new behaviors to familiar ones, individuals can leverage the power of automaticity and make change easier.

Linking Desired Behaviors: The key to successful habit stacking is linking desired behaviors to the existing routines. By clearly identifying the connection between the new behaviors and the anchor habits, individuals understand how to incorporate the desired changes into their daily lives.

Small Steps and Progression: Habit stacking emphasizes starting with small, achievable steps and gradually building upon them. This incremental approach helps individuals overcome resistance and build momentum towards lasting change.

Continuous Learning and Adaptation: Habit stacking is a dynamic process that requires continuous learning and adaptation. Individuals should regularly reflect on their habits, seek feedback, and adjust based on insights and changing circumstances.

Positive Reinforcement: Positive reinforcement plays a crucial role in habit stacking. Celebrating successes, recognizing progress, and providing rewards or incentives reinforce the desired behaviors and motivate individuals to continue practicing them.

Strategies for Change Management

Create a Compelling Vision: A compelling vision inspires individuals to embrace change. It should clearly communicate the purpose, benefits, and desired outcomes of the change initiative.

Establish Clear Goals and Objectives: Clear goals and objectives provide a roadmap for the change journey. They help individuals understand what is expected and track progress towards the desired outcomes.

Foster Stakeholder Engagement: Engaging stakeholders creates a sense of ownership and commitment. Involve stakeholders in decision-making, provide opportunities for input, and address their concerns throughout the change process.

Develop a Communication Plan: A well-defined communication plan ensures that key messages are effectively delivered to stakeholders. It should include multiple channels and emphasize two-way communication to facilitate understanding and address questions and concerns.

Provide Training and Support: Training programs and support mechanisms are vital for equipping individuals with the knowledge and skills required to adopt new behaviors. Offer resources, coaching, and mentoring to support individuals throughout their change journey.

Strategies for Habit Stacking

Identify Anchor Habits: Identify existing routines and habits that can serve as anchor habits for habit stacking. These anchor habits should be prevalent and relevant to the desired change behaviors.

Establish Habit Linkages: Clearly articulate the connection between the anchor habits and the desired behaviors. Highlight how the new behaviors complement and enhance the existing routines, making it easier for individuals to adopt and sustain the changes.

Provide Training and Education: Offer training programs and educational resources to help individuals understand the habit stacking process and develop the necessary skills to integrate new behaviors effectively.

Foster Accountability and Support: Establish mechanisms for tracking progress, providing feedback, and fostering accountability. Peer support, coaching, and recognition programs can encourage individuals to stay committed to habit stacking.

Encourage Reflection and Iteration: Encourage individuals to reflect on their habit stacking practices, learn from their experiences, and iterate their habits based on feedback and outcomes. Emphasize the importance of continuous improvement and adaptation.

Change management and habit stacking are powerful approaches for driving successful organizational change. By understanding and applying the key principles and strategies discussed throughout this book, organizations can create a solid foundation for change, leverage existing routines through habit stacking, and foster a culture of continuous improvement. The principles of change management, including clear vision, strong leadership, stakeholder engagement, effective communication, and adaptability, provide a framework for navigating change. Simultaneously, the principles of habit stacking, such as leveraging existing routines, linking desired behaviors, and reinforcing positive habits, offer a practical strategy for integrating new behaviors seamlessly into individuals' lives. By combining these approaches, organizations can drive meaningful and sustainable change, enhancing performance, productivity, and overall success. Embracing change and habit stacking as core components of organizational culture empowers individuals to adapt, innovate, and thrive in an ever-evolving business environment.

CHAPTER 28

THE POTENTIAL OF HABIT STACKING TO DRIVE MEANINGFUL ORGANIZATIONAL CHANGE

Habit stacking has gained recognition as a powerful technique for driving behavior change and fostering meaningful organizational transformation. By leveraging existing routines and habits, habit stacking enables individuals to seamlessly integrate new behaviors into their daily lives. This chapter explores the potential of habit stacking to drive meaningful organizational change, highlighting its benefits, applications, and key considerations for successful implementation.

Transforming Behavior at the Individual Level: Habit stacking has the potential to transform individual behavior within an organization. By linking desired behaviors to existing habits, individuals can adopt new behaviors more easily and sustain them over time. This approach overcomes the resistance and inertia often associated with change, allowing individuals to make gradual progress and build momentum towards meaningful transformation.

Cultivating a Culture of Change: Habit stacking, when applied organization-wide, has the power to cultivate a culture of change within an organization. By encouraging individuals at all levels to engage in habit stacking, organizations can create a collective mindset of continuous improvement and adaptability. This culture of change fosters innovation, agility, and resilience, positioning the organization for long-term success in a dynamic business environment.

Driving Employee Engagement and Empowerment: Habit stacking empowers employees by providing them with a structured approach to adopt new behaviors and contribute to organizational change. When employees are actively engaged in the habit stacking process, they feel a sense of ownership and control over their own development and the success of the organization. This empowerment enhances employee satisfaction, motivation, and overall engagement.

Improving Productivity and Performance: Habit stacking can significantly improve productivity and performance within an organization. By integrating new behaviors into daily routines, individuals can streamline processes, enhance efficiency, and optimize their workflow. The repetition and automaticity developed through habit stacking enable individuals to perform tasks more effectively and consistently, resulting in improved productivity and performance outcomes.

Enhancing Collaboration and Teamwork: Habit stacking can facilitate collaboration and teamwork by aligning behaviors and routines across individuals and teams. When teams engage in habit stacking together, they develop shared practices, rituals, and communication patterns. This synchronization fosters effective collaboration, strengthens relationships, and enhances overall teamwork within the organization.

Fostering Innovation and Creativity: Habit stacking provides a structured framework for fostering innovation and creativity within organizations. By integrating new habits related to experimentation, idea generation, and continuous learning, individuals are encouraged to think outside the box, explore new possibilities, and challenge the status quo. This mindset of innovation drives organizational growth and adaptability in a rapidly changing business landscape.

Supporting Change Initiatives and Organizational Goals: Habit stacking aligns with and supports broader change initiatives and organizational goals. Whether it is implementing a new technology, improving communication, or fostering a customer-centric culture, habit stacking can be tailored to address specific change objectives. By linking desired behaviors to these objectives, habit stacking reinforces the change initiatives and propels the organization towards its strategic goals.

Promoting Continuous Improvement: At its core, habit stacking promotes continuous improvement within organizations. The iterative nature of habit stacking allows individuals and teams to reflect on their habits, learn from experiences, and adjust as needed. This culture of continuous improvement enables organizations to stay agile, adapt to changing circumstances, and consistently refine their practices for better outcomes.

Key Considerations for Successful Implementation

To fully realize the potential of habit stacking in driving meaningful organizational change, certain considerations must be considered:

Clear Alignment: Ensure that the desired behaviors targeted through habit stacking align with the organization's vision, values, and strategic goals. Clear alignment ensures that habit stacking contributes to meaningful change and supports the overall direction of the organization.

Leadership Support: Obtain leadership support and commitment to habit stacking initiatives. Leaders play a crucial role in modeling desired behaviors, providing resources and support, and fostering a culture of change and habit stacking.

Communication and Training: Effective communication and training programs are essential for successful habit stacking implementation. Clearly communicate the purpose, benefits, and expectations of habit stacking to all individuals within the organization. Provide comprehensive training to equip individuals with the knowledge and skills required for habit stacking.

Measurement and Evaluation: Establish mechanisms for measuring and evaluating the impact of habit stacking initiatives. Define clear metrics and collect relevant data to assess the effectiveness and progress of habit stacking. Use this data to make data-driven decisions, refine strategies, and continuously improve the habit stacking process.

Sustainability and Integration: Ensure that habit stacking becomes a sustainable practice within the organization. Integrate habit stacking into performance management systems, talent development programs, and organizational routines to embed it as a core component of the organizational culture.

Immense Potential of Habit Stacking to Drive Meaningful Organizational Change

By leveraging existing routines and habits, habit stacking transforms behavior at the individual level, cultivates a culture of change, empowers employees, improves productivity and performance, enhances collaboration and teamwork. Habit stacking also fosters innovation and creativity, supports change initiatives, and promotes continuous improvement. By considering key implementation considerations and leveraging the benefits of habit stacking, organizations can harness its potential to drive meaningful and lasting change. Embracing habit stacking as a core component of the organizational culture empowers individuals, enhances organizational agility, and positions the organization for success in a rapidly evolving business landscape.

CHAPTER 29

FINAL THOUGHTS FOR LEADERS ON HARNESSING THE POWER OF HABIT STACKING

Throughout this book, we have explored the principles, strategies, and potential of habit stacking as a powerful tool for driving meaningful organizational change. As a leader, you hold the key to unlocking the full potential of habit stacking within your organization. In this final chapter, we will provide some concluding thoughts and a call to action for leaders to harness the power of habit stacking and drive transformative change.

Recognize the Power of Habits

As a leader, it is essential to recognize the power of habits in shaping behavior and driving change. Habits operate on a subconscious level and can have a significant impact on individual and organizational performance. By leveraging the existing habits of your employees through habit stacking, you can facilitate the adoption of new behaviors and drive meaningful change.

Lead by Example

Leadership by example is crucial when it comes to habit stacking. Embrace habit stacking practices yourself and openly communicate about your experiences, challenges, and successes. By demonstrating your commitment to habit stacking, you inspire and motivate others to follow suit. Your actions as a leader have a ripple effect on the organization, so lead by example and create a culture that values and embraces habit stacking.

Foster a Learning Culture

Creating a learning culture is essential to harnessing the power of habit stacking. Encourage continuous learning, experimentation, and innovation within your organization. Provide opportunities for employees to acquire new skills and knowledge that can be integrated into their habit stacking practices. Embrace a growth mindset and foster an environment where individuals feel safe to take risks, learn from failures, and continually improve.

Align Habit Stacking with Organizational Goals

To drive meaningful change, align habit stacking with your organization's goals and objectives. Identify the specific behaviors and habits that will contribute to the achievement of those goals. Clearly communicate the link between habit stacking and the organization's strategic direction, emphasizing how habit stacking supports the broader vision. This alignment creates a sense of purpose and ensures that habit stacking efforts are focused and impactful.

Invest in Training and Development

Investing in training and development is key to successful habit stacking implementation. Provide resources, workshops, and coaching to help employees understand the concept of habit stacking and develop the necessary skills to integrate new behaviors. Support employees in setting meaningful habits, monitoring progress, and adjusting as needed. By investing in their development, you empower your employees to drive their own growth and contribute to organizational change.

Embrace Feedback and Continuous Improvement

Feedback and continuous improvement are essential elements of habit stacking. Create a feedback-rich environment where individuals can reflect on their habit stacking practices and receive constructive input. Encourage regular check-ins and performance discussions that focus on habit stacking progress. Embrace a culture of continuous improvement, where individuals are encouraged to iterate and refine their habits based on feedback and lessons learned.

Celebrate Successes and Recognize Efforts

Celebrating successes and recognizing efforts is crucial to sustaining momentum and motivation. Acknowledge and celebrate the achievements of individuals and teams who have successfully integrated new behaviors through habit stacking. Recognize their efforts and the positive impact they have made on the organization. By celebrating successes, you reinforce the value of habit stacking and inspire others to embrace change.

Encourage Collaboration and Peer Support

Promote collaboration and peer support in habit stacking initiatives. Encourage employees to share their experiences, challenges, and insights with one another. Facilitate cross-functional collaboration, where individuals from different departments can learn from each other's habit stacking practices. Encourage the formation of peer support networks or buddy systems to foster accountability and motivation.

Evaluate and Measure Impact

To ensure the effectiveness of habit stacking initiatives, regularly evaluate and measure their impact. Define clear metrics and collect relevant data to assess the progress and outcomes of habit stacking efforts. Use this data to identify areas for improvement, make data-driven decisions, and continuously refine your habit stacking strategies.

Continuously Reinforce and Embed Habit Stacking

Habit stacking should not be a one-time initiative but rather an ongoing practice embedded in the fabric of your organization. Continuously reinforce the importance of habit stacking and integrate it into various aspects of your organization's operations. Embed habit stacking in performance management systems, talent development programs, and daily routines. By making habit stacking a part of your organizational DNA, you ensure its long-term sustainability and impact.

Harnessing the power of habit stacking as a leader is a transformative endeavor that can drive meaningful change within your organization. By recognizing the power of habits, leading by example, fostering a learning culture, aligning habit stacking with organizational goals, investing in training and development, embracing feedback and continuous improvement, celebrating successes, encouraging collaboration, evaluating, and measuring impact, and continuously reinforcing habit stacking, you can unlock the full potential of this approach.

As a leader, you can shape the behaviors, culture, and success of your organization. By embracing habit stacking and empowering your employees to adopt new behaviors, you create a culture of continuous improvement, innovation, and adaptability. So, embrace the power of habit stacking, lead with intention, and drive transformative change within your organization. The potential is vast, and the rewards are substantial. Act now and harness the power of habit stacking to shape a brighter future for your organization.

About the Author....Corey Stephenson

Corey Stephenson, entrepreneur, and non-fiction author, recognized for her expertise in personal development and unlocking the potential for lasting change. With her first book, "The Power of Habit Stacking: Unlock Your Potential for Lasting Change," Corey has become a respected authority in the field of habit formation, change management and personal growth.

With Corey's second book, "The Power of Habit Stacking: Change Management and Organizational Change", Corey explores organizations' constant need to adapt and embrace change. Whether it's the introduction of new technologies, shifts in market dynamics, or internal restructuring, change management has become a crucial discipline for success. However, implementing change within an organization can be a complex and challenging process. That's where the concept of habit stacking comes into play – a powerful strategy that can catalyze change and drive organizational growth.

Change management, at its core, is about guiding individuals, teams, and entire organizations through the process of transition. It entails understanding the current state, envisioning the desired future state, and strategically bridging the gap between them. While change can be disruptive and met with resistance, it also presents opportunities for innovation, improvement, and competitive advantage.

Enter habit stacking, a concept rooted in the understanding that lasting change is often best achieved by leveraging existing habits and routines. Habit stacking involves building upon existing behaviors to create new, desired habits. It recognizes that humans are creatures of habit, and by consciously linking new actions to established ones, the likelihood of successful adoption and integration increases significantly.

Corey's professional accomplishments and diverse background have played a significant role in shaping her unique perspective on self-improvement. Armed with a Master's in Strategic Management (MSM) and certifications as a Project Management Professional (PMP), Agile Certified Practitioner (PMI-ACP), and Certified Scrum Master, Corey brings a wealth of knowledge and experience to her work.

Throughout her career, Corey has worked with individuals and organizations, helping them identify and break through limiting patterns and habits. Her comprehensive understanding of project management and agile methodologies enables her to approach personal development in a systematic and strategic manner, providing readers with practical tools and techniques to transform their lives.

"The Power of Habit Stacking" serves as a culmination of Corey's extensive research, combining insights from psychology, neuroscience, and behavioral science to offer a powerful framework for lasting change. Her book guides readers through the process of habit stacking, a method that involves building upon existing routines to create positive and transformative habits. Corey's writing is clear, concise, and accessible, making complex concepts easily understandable for readers of all backgrounds.

As a sought-after mentor and speaker, Corey has shared her expertise with diverse audiences, including corporate teams, educational institutions, and personal development conferences. Her passion for helping others unlock their potential shines through in her engaging and thought-provoking presentations.

Corey's dedication to her craft extends beyond her writing and speaking engagements. She actively supports individuals in their personal development journeys, offering coaching and mentorship to guide them toward achieving their goals. Her commitment to empowering others to create lasting change has earned her a loyal following of readers and clients alike.

"The Power of Habit Stacking" has garnered widespread acclaim, earning praise from readers and experts in the field of personal development. Corey Stephenson's impact on the lives of individuals and the organizations she works with is a testament to her expertise and her genuine desire to help others unlock their true potential. As she continues to inspire and guide others on their personal growth journeys, Corey remains at the forefront of the self-improvement movement, leaving a legacy through her work.